Carol Shick

# Henry Trubner

# ROYAL ONTARIO MUSEUM

# The Far Eastern Collection

The Royal Ontario Museum, 1968

Design: William Rueter / Leslie Smart & Associates

Printed in Canada by The Hunter Rose Company

Publication of this Handbook is made possible through a grant generously provided by the J. P. Bickell Foundation.

## HALF TITLE

1 CEREMONIAL VESSEL (kuang)
*Shang Dynasty, An-yang period, c. 1300-1028 B.C. Reportedly from An-yang, and one of a group of vessels which Bishop White termed the 'Elephant Tomb' group.*
*Bronze H. 8 in. (20.3 cm.); l. 9 7/16 in. (24 cm.) Bishop White Collection, 933.12.52*

In the Shang and Western Chou periods complicated bird and animal shapes were given to a number of vessels, particularly to the water vessel called *kuang*. The animal whose head appears on the lid of this example has been identified as a Muntjac deer because of its distinctive horns. The small elephants seen near the base of the spout on the body, and also found on other vessels from the same find, have given this 'Elephant Tomb' group its name.

PUBL.: *Illustrated London News*, May 18, 1935, Pl. IV, Fig. 2; C. Hentze, *Bronzegerät, Kultbauten, Religion im ältesten China der Shang-zeit*, Antwerp, 1951, Pls. LXIV, LXV; W. C. White, *Bronze Culture of Ancient China*, Toronto, 1956, Pl. V; L. Davidson, 'The Riddle of the Bottle Horn,' *Artibus Asiae*, Vol. XXII 1959, Fig. 7.

## FRONTISPIECE

2 WALL PAINTING OF MAITREYA BUDDHA AND BODHISATTVAS
*Yüan Dynasty, first quarter of 14th century From Northern Hall of Hsing-hua-ssu ('Monastery of the Joyful Conversion'), Chi-shan, Southwest Shansi*
*Wall painting, water-base pigments over clay ground with mud-and-straw foundation Ht. 18 ft. 11 3/8 in. (5.77 m.); l. 38 ft. 2 1/8 in. (11.74 m.) 933.6.1*

Maitreya Buddha, seated upon throne in characteristic pose with both legs pendant, flanked by two Bodhisattvas, Manjusri to his left holding a book, and Samantabhadra on his right. The trinity of Maitreya is patterned after that of Śākyamuni, who is ordinarily accompanied by Manjusri and Samantabhadra. The two monks standing in the back again correspond to the companions of Śākyamuni, Ānanda and Kaśyapa. At either side a conversion scene is depicted, centred around legendary figures drawn from Buddhist scriptures associated with the coming of Maitreya. The scene on the left depicts the initiation into the Buddhist order of Brahmavati, mother of Maitreya, balanced on the opposite side by the initiation of King Sankha of Ketumati. Both the king and queen are being tonsured and are surrounded by attendants. The two conversion scenes are associated with the coming of Maitreya from the Tushita Heaven and the selection of his parents. The boy crying beside the king is the heir-apparent, who laments the fact that he has to remain a layman while his father becomes a monk. The child emerging from the folds of the lady's mantle is an allusion to the birth of Maitreya and is derived from the traditional scene of Queen Maya giving birth to Śākyamuni.

The style of the painting is related to a pair of Buddhist wall paintings in the University Museum, Philadelphia, a single wall painting in the Nelson Gallery – Atkins Museum, Kansas City, and a fourth related example in the Metropolitan Museum of Art, New York. The Philadelphia, Kansas City and New York paintings originate from the Lower Temple of the Kuang-shêng-ssu, also in southwest Shansi, but somewhat to the north of the Hsing-hua-ssu, whence come the Toronto paintings. On the basis of available evidence, it can be assumed that the four paintings from the Kuang-shêng-ssu are from the first half of the fourteenth century, probably the second quarter. The mural in the Royal Ontario Museum, which is stylistically slightly earlier, dates from about 1300. The composition of the Toronto painting is quite similar to the others, but the designs are somewhat simpler, and the lines calmer and less fluid. An inscription 'on the wall' written by the artist and found *in situ* by two students working for Bishop White, contains a cyclical date which can be read as 1298, as well as several other cyclical combinations falling within the first half of the fourteenth century. The exact date remains uncertain, though there is no doubt that the painting is a product of the first half, probably the first quarter, of the fourteenth century.

CF. *Pei-ching ta hsüeh yen chiu so kuo hsüeh men yüeh k'an* (Bulletin de l'institut de sinologie de l'université nationale de Pekin), Vol. I, No. 1, Shanghai, 1926, pp. 1-7; *Philadelphia Museum Journal*, University of Pennsylvania, Sept., 1926; June, 1928; June, 1929; L. Sickman, 'Wall Paintings of the Yüan Period in Kuang-shêng-ssu,' *Revue des Arts Asiatiques*, Vol. XI, June, 1937, pp. 53-67.

PUBL.: W.C. White, *Chinese Temple Frescoes, A Study of Three Wall-paintings of the Thirteenth Century*, Toronto, 1940; L. Bachhofer, ' "Maitreya in Katumati" by Chou Hao-ku,' *India Antiqua*, Leyden, 1947, pp. 1-7; O. Sirén, *Chinese Painting, Leading Masters and Principles*, Vol. VI, London, 1958, pls. 1-2; A. Guiganino, *La Pittura Cinese*, Rome, 1959, Pl. 271; T.A. Heinrich, *Art Treasures in the Royal Ontario Museum*, Toronto, 1963, pp. 33-39; A. Lippe, 'Buddha and the Holy Multitude,' *The Metropolitan Museum of Art Bulletin*, May, 1965, Pl. 1, pp. 325-336.

# Contents

3 BOWL ON HIGH FOOT
*Shang or Early Chou Dynasty, c. 1300-900 B.C.
Gray pottery  H. 8 1/2 in. (21.5 cm.); dia. (at mouth) 11 7/8 in.
(03.2 cm.)  960.238.39*

Large bowl of unglazed gray ware, wheel made, with everted lip, rounded sides and high foot. Decorated inside and outside near rim with incised horizontal lines; three rings around exterior of foot. Design of incised triangles below rings encircling rim. Between triangles and rim are three heads in low relief, resembling the *t'ao-t'ieh*. Gray pottery, often found at neolithic sites, is the oldest type of pottery indigenous to China, in contrast to painted or black pottery, which is believed to have been introduced to China from the West.

CF. *Sekai Kōkogaku Taikei*, Vol. 6, Tokyo, 1959, pp. 111-112, Fig. 325; *Sekai Tōji Zenshū*, Vol. 8, Tokyo, 1955, p. 194, Fig. 64 and p. 190; W. Watson, *Archaeology in China*, London, 1960, Pl. 51.

The preparation and editing of this Handbook have been the responsibility of Henry Trubner, the Curator of the Museum's Far Eastern Department from 1958 to 1968, assisted by Mrs. Barbara Stephen and Miss Haruko Tsuchiya, Assistant Curators in the Department. Miss Ann Glyn, Technician, has been responsible for checking the dimensions of the objects and other data. All photographs are the work of Mr. Leighton Warren, Royal Ontario Museum Photographer. Without their untiring help and assistance the realization of this Handbook could not have been achieved.

ABBREVIATIONS

The following abbreviations have been used in the text:
*Archives*: Archives of the Chinese Art Society of America
B.M.F.E.A.: Bulletin of the Museum of Far Eastern Antiquities
T.O.C.S.: Transactions of the Oriental Ceramic Society

**4** HOLLOW PILLAR
*Later Han Dynasty, 1st-2nd century* A.D.
*Gray pottery   H. 43 9/16 in. (110.6 cm.)   925.26.90*

Pillar hexagonal in cross-section, with two bevelled edges in front, and surmounted by a demon figure in full round. Legs in relief on sides with arms placed around upper part of pillar. The decoration consists of narrow vertical and horizontal bands with dragons, as well as geometric and abstract designs.
Hollow pillars of this type were used during the Han period in the construction of underground tombs and offering chambers. As in the case of the Han tiles, the decoration was applied by means of stamp moulds.

Similar pillars, crowned by demoniac figures, have been published by O. Jansé, *Briques et objects céramiques funeraires de l'époque des Han, appartenant à C.T. Loo et Cie*, Paris, 1936, Pl XXIII, Figs. 1 a, 1 b, and in *Chinese Sculpture*, Collection of Jan Kleijkamp and Ellis Monroe, the M.H. de Young Memorial Museum, San Francisco, 1944, Pl. III. See also *Arts of the Han Dynasty*, Chinese Art Society of America, Asia House, New York, 1961, No. 6.

# Introduction

The Royal Ontario Museum's collection of Far Eastern art and archaeology occupies an entire wing of about twenty galleries on the Museum's third floor. In addition, three Chinese wall paintings, outstanding in size and importance, and several examples of Buddhist sculpture are shown in a large gallery on the main floor. The Museum's particularly rich and extensive holdings of Chinese art and archaeology are well known to scholars throughout the world. The Far Eastern collection also includes many important and representative examples of Indian and Japanese art.

The collection of Chinese art and archaeology is one of the largest and most important of its kind, and its unique character distinguishes it from other collections outside of the Chinese mainland. It is primarily the result of the activities of two men, George Crofts and, after his death in 1925, William Charles White, Anglican Bishop of Honan. With the help and assistance of the Museum's first Director, Dr. Charles Trick Currelly, these men were able to secure in China, during the 1920s and early thirties respectively, the greater part of what constitutes the present Chinese collection. At a time when Chinese art was still little known to the western world, Dr. Currelly committed himself and the Museum to the acquisition of enormous quantities of Chinese works of art and rare archaeological material, without ever knowing where the money would come from to pay for the huge shipments arriving from China in a steady stream. The amazing result is that Toronto today has one of the world's truly great collections of Chinese art, a collection so unique and so varied that it will be impossible ever again to bring together such a remarkable group of objects.

George Crofts and Bishop White were fortunate to be in China at a time when a great many objects were unearthed from tombs in various parts of the country. Unfortunately, these early excavations were haphazard and not scientifically controlled as they would be today. Many important objects were nevertheless brought to light, usually as the result of clandestine excavations. Thanks to the foresight and initiative of these two men, large quantities of this material subsequently found their way into the Royal Ontario Museum. The deep interest and enthusiastic support of Dr. Currelly was aided by the generosity of a number of private donors, notably Mr. and Mrs. H. D. Warren, who provided the financial means which enabled the Museum to acquire the objects arriving from China. Many other donors, notably Sir Edmund

Walker, Major and Mrs. James E. Hahn and Mrs. Edgar J. Stone, have helped the Far Eastern Department substantially over the years.

The collection of ancient Chinese ritual bronzes and other Shang and Chou artifacts, the Wei and T'ang pottery tomb figures, and the ceramic vessels of the T'ang and Sung Dynasties are among the finest of their kind. The Chinese collection, in particular, is so renowned, and at the same time so rare and unusual, that scholars and connoisseurs come from all parts of the world to see it. Because of its vast reserves, the collection is also a major source of inspiration to students of Far Eastern art. It opens up unique possibilities for research and advanced studies, for it is one of the major sources in the west where the art and archaeology of ancient China may be studied first-hand, on the basis of original and often unpublished material.

The Chinese collection differs in content from other museum collections in the west in that it is not solely oriented towards ancient Chinese art. Considerable emphasis is also placed upon the archaeology of early China. The collection of ritual bronzes, for example, which is largely the result of the activities of Bishop White, was not assembled from an aesthetic or collector's point of view. The individual objects, on the contrary, were often selected for archaeological reasons in an attempt to present as complete a picture as possible of the material culture of the Shang and Chou civilizations. The many bronze vessels of this period are therefore supplemented by important study material such as moulds for bronze castings, legs, handles and other fragments which are highly significant for the investigation of Shang and Chou bronze technology. There are also large numbers of weapons, horse and chariot fittings and various other artifacts.

Dr. James M. Menzies, a Christian missionary and later a student of Bishop White at the University of Toronto, resided for many years in the vicinity of An-yang, the ancient Shang capital. During this time he acquired a large number of rare Shang bronze objects – many of them fragmentary, but of unusual archaeological interest – as well as pottery, carved ivory, jade and stone objects and, most important of all, a very extensive collection of rare Shang Oracle Bones. The entire Menzies collection was acquired by the University of Toronto in 1960 and is now a permanent part of the museum's Far Eastern Collection.

Bishop White was succeeded as Curator of the Department

by Miss Helen E. Fernald. During this time, important additions were made to the collection. It is hoped that at some future date some of Miss Fernald's unpublished research and her important contributions to knowledge about the Far Eastern Collection may be published.

The museum's enormous collection of pottery tomb figures is likewise without rival in the west. George Crofts was responsible for acquiring the bulk of this material in China during the period from 1918-1925. The Wei figures, especially the two Funerary Processions (Pl. 43) are rare and unusual, but the collection of tomb figures includes many other important examples covering the centuries from the Han to the Ming Dynasty. The tomb figures not only shed much light on the burial practices of ancient China but also provide a vast amount of information concerning the dress, customs and manners of various periods. Preliminary work towards an eventual catalogue of the tomb figures has already been done by Miss Fernald.

The collection also includes an unusually large representation of Chinese ceramics, ranging from examples of neolithic painted pottery to the finished products of the Ming and Ch'ing Dynasties. The green glazed pottery of the Han Dynasty, covered with a simple lead-silicate glaze (Pl. 12, 40, 41), T'ang polychromes with characteristic splashed and mottled glazes (Pl. 53), and the elegant, refined monochromes of the Sung Dynasty (Pl. 70-72) are illustrated by many exceptionally fine examples. The student of Chinese ceramics will find here many important and characteristic types showing the development of the potter's art in China, already very advanced at an early date. Proto-porcelain was produced at least as early as the Han Dynasty (Pl. 38, 39), and true porcelain was made by the T'ang potters more than a thousand years before the first firing of pure porcelain in Europe (Pl. 56).

Among the ceramic products of the later periods, the collection of Ming and early Ch'ing blue-and-white porcelains is especially noteworthy. It includes a number of important examples from the fifteenth and sixteenth centuries (Pl. 83-85), and an unusually large and interesting group of blue-and-whites from the Transition period, the era between the end of Wan-li, in 1620, and the year 1683, in the reign of K'ang-hsi, when kilns were once again established under imperial patronage at Ching-tê-chên.

Buddhism, which reached China as early as the first cen-

tury A.D., did not become a force of major influence in the Middle Kingdom until the conquest of the Wei or Toba Tartars who in 386 settled at Ta-t'ung-fu in northern Shansi, made it their capital, and established the Wei Dynasty. The Wei people adopted Buddhism as their official state religion. Under their patronage, Buddhist art soon entered upon a period of great florescence, as witnessed by the magnificent sculptures from the Buddhist cave-temples at Yün-Kang, outside of Ta-t'ung-fu, and Lung-mên, near Lo-yang.

Chinese scupture came into its own during the centuries following the introduction of Buddhism. Particularly noteworthy in the ROM collection are the Buddhist stele, from the early sixth century (Pl. 45), the side of a Mortuary Bed, a work of the second half of the sixth century (Pl. 49), the dated Northern Ch'i marble figure of Amitabha (Pl. 47), the stone Demon from Hsiang-t'ang Shan, also of Northern Ch'i date (Pl. 46) and the Bodhisattva from T'ien-lung Shan, striking in its relaxed pose and sensuous modelling, the result of strong Indian influence (Pl. 48). Stone sculpture declined rapidly in China after the end of the T'ang Dynasty, in the ninth century, but the collection has an unusually large number of wooden figures, mostly from the Shansi-Shensi region, where isolated pockets of wood sculpture continued to flourish under the Mongol Liao and Chin Dynasties. The two dated statues of Kuan-yin and Ta-shih-chih are rare and important examples of this later type of Chinese sculpture (Pl. 75).

In its original form Buddhism centred around the life of the historical Buddha, Śākyamuni, who lived in eastern India, in the Ganges Valley, where he wandered about preaching the doctrine and performing miracles. During the Kushan and Gupta periods, from about the first to the sixth century A.D., Buddhism became the dominant spiritual and political force in India, and subsequently spread to south-east Asia and eastward through Central Asia to China and ultimately to Korea and Japan. The Kushan and Gupta periods also represent the high point of Buddhist art in India.

It is generally believed that the earliest examples of Buddhist sculpture, showing the Buddha in human form, were made towards the end of the first century A.D. in the ancient province of Gandhāra, comprising present Northwest Pakistan and Afghanistan. Gandhāra was originally a province of the Iranian empire of the Achaemenids. About A.D. 50 the

Kushans, a race of eastern Central Asian origin, established their rule over the Gandhāra region. They were in close commercial and diplomatic contact with the West, and the artisans who worked in the various religious establishments of the Kushan kingdom were at first journeying craftsmen from such eastern Roman outposts as Antioch and Alexandria.

The artistic affiliations of the Gandhāra school were with Rome, rather than Greece, and the earliest Buddhist images represent a combination of various elements of pagan art used by the foreign craftsmen to create an image of the Buddha. The merging of classical and Indian elements created a hybrid style of sculpture, local to this region. The principal contribution of the Gandhāra school to the art of Asia was the introduction of the Buddha image. The Gandhāra workshops also produced a Bodhisattva type, many of which undoubtedly depict Prince Siddhārta in the garments of a contemporary rajah.

The museum's collection of Indian and Pakistan art contains a number of fine and typical Gandhāra examples of the Buddha and Bodhisattya types, carved from the dark bluish-gray schist characteristic of Gandhāra sculpture (Pl. 112). The collection also includes a number of interesting Gandhāra reliefs, originally part of the decoration of Buddhist stupas and monasteries which abounded in this area. These reliefs, for the most part, illustrate Buddhist stories, scenes from the life of Śākyamuni or various miracles performed by him, as well as secular scenes (Pl. 113, 114).

Beginning in the third century, stone sculpture in the Gandhāra region declined in favour of images made of stucco. During the later phase of Gandhāra sculpture, the bodies of Buddhist figures were often modelled in mud and straw; when they disintegrated, only the stucco heads remained. The imposing head of a Bodhisattva (Pl. 111) is a characteristic example of this later phase. It is also one of the largest known stucco heads of this type and must originally have been part of a colossal statue.

The fragment of a stupa railing, carved in the red sandstone characteristic of the Mathurā school, is a fine example of Kushan sculpture (Pl. 115). Despite its small size and fragmentary nature, it reveals the technical refinement and skill of the Kushan sculptors. In the seventh century, following the breakup of the Gupta empire, Buddhism rapidly declined, and Hinduism came to take its place. Hereafter, only isolated pockets of Buddhism remained, notably in eastern India in Bihar and Bengal, where under the Pāla and Sena Dynasties (Pl. 116, 117) Buddhist art continued to flourish until the twelfth century.

The vitality and sensuousness of Hindu art are vividly shown by several fine examples of stone sculpture in the museum's collection, mostly from temples in central and southern India (Pl. 118, 119), and a superb thirteenth-to-fourteenth century Dancing Śiva (Natarāja) in bronze (Pl. 122). Among the Indian bronzes, the rare image of Chakrapurusa (Pl. 110) and the small figure of a yakshī or nature spirit (Pl. 120) are also particularly outstanding.

Japan was a relative late-comer in the rising cultural pattern of the Far East. Except for the Jōmon, Yayoi and other pre-Buddhist cultures, primarily devoted to the production of pottery objects, Japanese art did not come fully into being until the introduction of Buddhism about the middle of the sixth century. The first official mention of Buddhism occurs in the *Nihongi* for the year 552. Buddhism at first faced heavy odds in Japan and its progress was slow until it found an official champion in the devout Prince Shōtoku. In 593, when the Empress Suiko ascended the throne, Shōtoku Taishi was made regent and the position of Buddhism was thereafter secure. He dedicated himself to the task of propagating the new faith throughout the land and, in 604, he promulgated a series of decrees establishing Buddhism as the official state religion. The great temples such as Hōryū-ji, near Nara, became centres of learning and of Buddhist teaching.

Buddhist art also spread rapidly in the course of the seventh century, as witnessed by the increasing numbers of Buddhist temples and images. It reached its zenith in the Tempyō period, in the eighth century, a time of intense religious fervour and great artistic achievements, corresponding to the T'ang period in China and the Gupta period in India. But while Buddhism declined in India and China following the breakup of the Gupta and T'ang empires, the Tempyō period was only the high point in a long period of florescence of Buddhist art in Japan, extending from the Asuka period in the seventh century to the Buddhist renaissance of the Kamakura period, in the thirteenth and early fourteenth century.

The museum's collection of Japanese art, although small in size when compared to the Chinese holdings, contains a number of important objects, most of them acquired in recent years. Two outstanding examples of sculpture, one Buddhist, the other Shinto, illustrate the remarkable qualities of Heian period sculpture (tenth-twelfth centuries). The figure of Jizō (Pl. 100), a work of the tenth century, is an unusually fine example of the Heian style and was made in the *ichiboku* ('single wood block') technique. It illustrates the *hompa* or 'rolling wave' style of drapery folds, a characteristic feature of the ninth century Jōgan style carried over into the Heian period. The sculpture is distinguished by simple, rounded contours and the long, sweeping lines of the folds. It expresses a calm, serene mood. The simple treatment and deep spiritual quality reflect the highest achievements of Heian sculpture. The Shinto figure (Pl. 102), a work of the twelfth century, is likewise carved in the *ichiboku* technique, but contrasts with the image of Jizō in its stylized flatness and sharper, almost angular carving.

Two very fine heads which originally formed part of a statue of Jūichimen Kannon (Eleven-headed Kannon) are the generous gift of Mrs. Edgar J. Stone. The heads, which are iconographically most interesting, are products of the late tenth to eleventh centuries (Pl. 101).

Japanese Buddhist painting is represented in the collection by a superb example of the Taima Mandara. It dates from the Kamakura period and is one of the earliest and best versions of this famous subject outside Japan. The painting, a work of the second half of the thirteenth century, depicts the paradise of Amida Buddha, ruler of the Western Paradise (Pl. 104). The painting follows a traditional composition, going back to the original Tempyō version of the Taima Mandara, very much damaged and owned by Taima-dera. The ROM's example is distinguished by firm line drawing, great delicacy of individual details and brilliant colouring overlaid in *kirikane* ('cut-gold'). It is one of the outstanding examples of Kamakura religious painting.

This type of composition, showing Amida's land of bliss and happiness, became very popular under the influence of the Jōdō (Pure Land) sect. The Jōdō sect of Buddhism, founded by the Chinese priest Shên-tao, was brought to Japan by Priest Eshin. It taught that asceticism was not the answer to salvation but that man could be reborn in the Western Paradise, or Pure Land of Amida, simply by having faith in Amida and his powers of salvation. This teaching, with its emphasis on an easy path to salvation, had wide appeal and gave rise to the increasing popularity in the Kamakura period of painted mandaras, depicting the paradise of Amida.

Examples of narrative scrolls, a type of painting in which Japanese artists excelled, are unfortunately lacking in the collection, as are other important forms of Japanese pictorial art. There are, however, two fine examples of Japanese decorative painting, which emerged as a major artistic expression in the Momoyama and Early Edo periods, in the late seventeenth and early eighteenth century, when artists were called upon to decorate the elaborate residences of rulers and feudal lords. Two fine pairs of screens in the collection, products of the eighteenth century, provide at least a glimpse of the richness and variety of later Japanese decorative painting. The Flower Cart screens (Pl. 108) are a characteristic work of the Edo period, striking in the abstract nature of the composition and strong colouring against a brilliant gold background.

The screens by Itō Jakuchū, representing chickens and flowering plum branches, have only recently been added to the collection (Pl. 107). In contrast to the Flower Cart screens they are remarkable in their powerful monochrome effects, both in the skilful use of *sumi-e* ('ink-painting') and in the simplicity of the individual composition. Strong accents of black ink are ingeniously contrasted with the surrounding white areas of the paper. The painting follows the ancient tradition of ink painting, developed in the fifteenth and sixteenth century under the influence of Chinese painting of the Yüan and Ming Dynasties, and under the impact of Zen Buddhism, which favoured simple and direct means of expression. At the same time, the rendering is very modern in concept, in the abstract treatment, and abbreviated yet powerful pictorial effect.

The Royal Ontario Museum's Far Eastern Collection, briefly described in the preceding paragraphs, is unusual in scope and quality and is one of the most remarkable collections of its kind. Especially in the field of Chinese art and archaeology, it occupies a place of unique importance among museum collections in the West. In an effort to make the contents of this rare collection more understandable and to bring knowledge of some of the more significant objects to a larger number of scholars, interested students, and to a wider public, this illustrated Handbook of the collection has been prepared.

Henry Trubner
Curator, Far Eastern Department

# The Bronze Age

5 CEREMONIAL VESSEL *(fang-i)*
*Shang Dynasty, An-yang period, c. 1300-1028 B.C.*
Bronze   H. 9 5/8 in. (24.4 cm.)   955.66

Large *t'ao-t'ieh* mask on each side and narrow band above and below, decorated respectively with confronted birds and dragons. *T'ao-t'ieh* mask on each side of cover in upside down position. Background filled with *lei-wên* design of round and square spirals. Knob on cover and notched flanges at corners and dividing each side of body as well as cover.
The *fang-i* belongs to a group of square or rectangular forms which were popular in the An-yang period. It has been suggested that such forms developed from slab-sided wooden prototypes, whereas the rounded vessels reflect ceramic shapes. Whatever its derivation, the *fang-i* provides a good surface for the large *t'ao-t'ieh* masks and confronted bird and animal designs which usually decorate it.

CF. P. Ackerman, *Ritual Bronzes of Ancient China*, New York, 1945, Pl. 60; B. Karlgren, 'Bronzes in the Wessen Collection,' *B.M.F.E.A.*, Vol. 30, 1958, Pl. 1.

PUBL.: T A. Heinrich, *Art Treasures in the Royal Ontario Museum*, Toronto, 1963, p. 31.

The art of China, spanning more than 4,000 years, is the product of one of the oldest and richest civilizations known to man. Chinese art is not only distinct from that of her neighbours, but has no parallels in the art of the Middle East and Europe. After two millennia its influence spread to permeate the arts of Korea and Japan.

Some items in the ROM collection of Chinese art precede documented history. Two splendid examples of pottery jars (Pl. 14, 15) from neolithic times are prized objects. They are dated some time before 1523 B.C. – before the Shang established the first recorded dynasty of China. The jars are painted pottery decorated with spiral and zoomorphic designs. They were found in far western China in Kansu Province at the site of Pan-shan and are typical of the florescence of the neolithic Painted Pottery style.

Some of the rarest and most important objects in the Chinese collection are the large number of bronze vessels, weapons, fittings of bronze and jade, and other artifacts from the Shang and Chou Dynasties. The collection of ritual bronzes includes most, if not all, of the important types and shapes. A large reservoir of additional vessels, not always on exhibition, is available to students and other interested persons. They range in time from the powerful yet simple shapes and designs of the Shang Dynasty (1523-1028 B.C.) through the often more elaborate and complex examples of the Chou period (1027-222 B.C.) to culminate in the more decorative, elegant vessels, sometimes with inlay of precious metals, of the Late Chou and Han Dynasties (c. 600 B.C.-A.D. 220).

Until 1950 evidence for the material culture of the Shang Dynasty was based upon the finds from the An-yang region, in Honan, site of the Shang capital from c. 1300-1028 B.C. Nothing was then known of earlier sites, which might antedate the An-yang, or Late Shang, phase of Shang civilization. The discovery, a few years ago, of important finds in the districts of Chêng-chou and Hui-hsien in Honan, and at Huang-p'i in Hopei, has established the existence of an apparent pre-An-yang bronze culture, but there is as yet very little definite knowledge of the Middle Shang period. Nor have the excavations of the Middle Shang sites so far brought to light any inscribed or dated material. Much of our present knowledge, including the dating of the so-called pre-An-yang bronzes (of which a number are in the ROM collection), is still conjectural. Attempts have been made to identify Chêng-chou with the ancient city of Ao, second capital of the Shang

6 CEREMONIAL VESSEL (tsun)
*Shang Dynasty, An-yang period, c. 1300-1028 B.C.*
*Bronze H. 13 3/4 in. (34.9 cm.) Purchased with funds from the*
*Reuben Wells Leonard Bequest, 954.136.2*

The decorative motifs of dissolved t'ao-t'ieh masks contained within narrow bands round the shoulder and body are similar to the designs on a number of small, early bronzes recently uncovered in China and believed to date from a period earlier than the main occupation of An-yang. The size of this tsun, however, and the solidity of its form suggest a date after the beginning of the An-yang period, probably in the thirteenth century B.C.

PUBL.: Tch'ou Tö-yi, *Bronzes Antiques de la Chine Appartenant à C.T. Loo et Cie.*, Paris, 1924 Pl. XVI; S. Umehara, *Shina Kodō Seikwa*, Part I, Vol. I, Osaka, 1933, Pl. 33; B. Karlgren, 'New Studies on Chinese Bronzes,' B.M.F.E.A. Vol. 9, 1937, Pl. LI, No. 759; H. E. Fernald, 'Six Bronze Vessels from China,' *R.O.M.A. Bulletin*, No. 23, May, 1955, Fig. 1; B. Karlgren, 'Marginalia on some Bronze Albums: II,' B.M.F.E.A., Vol. 32, 1960, Pl. 25 a.

Dynasty, but strong objections against this theory have also been raised. For the time being the question of the possible identity of Chêng-chou with the capital city of Ao must be left open. Despite these uncertainties, a number of vessels in the museum, not illustrated here, and mostly of the *chüeh*, *chia* and *ku* types, have tentatively been assigned to a pre-An-yang phase of Shang art. Even these vessels, already advanced in technique and decorative design, do not seem to represent the beginnings of the bronze art in China, but rather an already advanced stage of development.

The Shang state, centred around the capital city of An-yang, came to an end with the Chou conquest and establishment of the Chou Dynasty in 1027 B.C. The Chou people, who were evidently Chinese, had been settled in Shensi before their conquest. They were situated between the Shang in the east and various non-Chinese nomadic tribes in the north and northwest. The Chou came to Shang China not so much as conquerors but as a people eager to assimilate and accept the rich Shang civilization which was flourishing at An-yang. No lessening of artistic contributions occurred under the Chou, and workshops appear to have continued their activities despite the changed political conditions. Gradually the characteristic Shang shapes and decorative motifs underwent change, resulting in a distinctive Chou style of bronzes.

Under the Chou the important centre of culture shifted from An-yang to Lo-yang, also in Honan and a short distance away. The Lo-yang finds include bronze vessels, a large number of chariot and other fittings, belt-hooks, jade ornaments and pendants, glass beads and other artifacts. Many of the bronze articles show embellishments of gold, silver, turquoise or other inlays. Most of the Lo-yang material may be dated between the fifth and third centuries B.C., and shows the height of the Late Chou bronze style.

Curvilinear motifs and zoomorphic forms associated with the Shang style slowly gave way in favour of more purely geometric, conventionalized patterns, characteristic of the Middle Chou style. At the same time new shapes were introduced, while some of those popular during the Shang and Early Chou periods were discontinued. The Late Chou style saw a revival of some of the earlier patterns and shapes, although greatly modified. The severity and formalism of the Shang style were replaced by greater elegance and a growing sophistication in shape, and by a more predominantly decorative approach, augmented by the use of inlay in the designs and motifs.

With the advent of the Han Dynasty, worship of the ancestors and the ritual which accompanied it, so much in evidence during Shang and Early Chou, was superseded by a more material culture. As a result, the need for bronze vessels other than for purely decorative and materialistic purposes declined sharply. Pottery became more and more popular, particularly for household and funerary articles – witness the large quantities of Han pottery, of which the ROM has an extensive collection.

**7 HUMAN FIGURE**
*Late Chou Dynasty, 5th – 3rd century B.C. From Ch'ang-sha, Hunan Wood with traces of paint H. 21 3/8 in. (54.3 cm.); w. (at base) 4 17/32 in. (11.5 cm.)* 950.36.1

Tall male figure, roughly carved in wood, wearing a long mantle covering both shoulders. The figure is very flat with abstract rendering of face and body except for a few touches of carving in detail, such as ears, triangularly pointed nose and chin. The hands are hidden inside the sleeves in front. The hair, with pigtail, is typically Chinese in style; the face and costume are painted primarily in black, while traces of vermilion are visible on the mouth and at the edge of the collar. A roughly painted hook-like design in red is seen on the costume, while horizontal stripes on the sleeves and vertical stripes at the bottom of the garment are done in black. In the back of the figure there is a square area, left unpainted, the use of which is unknown.

The figure was found at Ch'ang-sha, in Hunan Province, South China, which was a flourishing city of the state of Ch'u during the Eastern Chou period. This type of figure was entombed for the purpose of exorcising demons and to serve the deceased after death. It belongs to a class of objects known as *ming-ch'i*, which were made for burial and acted as substitutes for real people and animals in the spirit world. Sacrificial death was commonly practised during Shang and Early Chou, and the making of substitutes in wood or clay thus represents an advance over the earlier, primitive practice.

CF. S. Mizuno, 'Chōsa shutsudo no mokugū ni tsuite,' (On the Wooden Figures Excavated from Ch'ang-sha), *Tōhō Gakuhō*, No. 8, Kyoto, 1937; *An Exhibition of Chinese Antiquities from Ch'ang-sha lent by J. H. Cox*, Yale University, 1939, Figs. 2-3; *Sekai Tōji Zenshū*, Vol. 8, Tokyo, 1955, pp. 252-253, Figs. 257, 258; *Sekai Bunkashi Taikei*, Vol. 15, *China (1)*, Tokyo, 1958, p. 134, Figs. 278, 280, 310, *Sekai Kōkogaku Taikei*, Vol. 6, Tokyo, 1959, Fig. 222; W. Watson, *Archaeology in China*, London, 1960, Pl. 97; T. Misugi, ed. *Old Chinese Art* (Chugoku Kinseki Toji Zukan Kauko-kao), Osaka, 1961, Pl. 34; *The Art of Eastern Chou*, Chinese Art Society of America, New York, 1962, No. 3; *Sekai Bijutsu Taikei*, Vol. 8, Chinese Art (1), Tokyo, 1963, p. 157, Fig. 17.

# Chinese Sculpture

Throughout the greater part of its history Chinese sculpture has been dominated by the powerful influence of the Buddhist faith and its artistic requirements. Most of the Chinese sculpture in the ROM collection is accordingly Buddhist in content, although there are earlier, pre-Buddhist examples, usually on a small scale – for instance, the Late Chou bronze figure from Chin-ts'un in Honan Province (Pl. 23), and the wood figure from Ch'ang-sha in Hunan (Pl. 7). Both are excellent examples of the earlier, still primitive stage of Chinese sculpture, before any monumental work in stone or wood had been produced. They postdate by several centuries the earliest extant examples of Chinese sculpture, illustrated by a number of human and animal sculptures of white marble from the site of the Shang capital at An-yang, and a ceremonial wine vessel in the form of a rhinoceros, also from this site, now in the Avery Brundage Collection at the M. H. de Young Museum, San Francisco.

The gray pottery tiles of the Han Dynasty, decorated with stamped designs of landscape, animal and figure motifs, provide important documentary evidence of the pictorial art of this period (Pl. 35). An early interest in nature and in the representation of landscape is even more clearly suggested by the subjects depicted on the Han reliefs from the tomb of General Tso Yüan-i, in the Li-shih district, Shansi (Pl. 37). They include a hunting scene in which figures on horseback and some on foot advance towards a mountain range on the left, and a second panel in which a procession of horsemen is separated from a hunting scene to the left by a large tree with massive foliage. Details of the foliage were originally reinforced in ink, traces of which still remain. The stone reliefs are important as examples of Han funerary sculpture and the use of landscape in composition. They also suggest that the themes depicted on them were derived from contemporary wall paintings, for the treatment is linear and pictorial rather than truly sculptural.

Knowledge of Buddhism probably reached China from India early in the Christian era, but the new religion did not exert any great influence upon Chinese culture until several centuries later. Buddhism began to play a major role with the arrival of the Wei or Toba Tartars in A.D. 386 and the establishment of the Northern Wei Dynasty. Very soon thereafter, the Wei began the hollowing out of countless Buddhist cave-temples from the sandstone cliffs at Yün-kang, not far from the Wei capital at Ta-t'ung-fu, in Shansi. Persecution of Buddhism, periodically initiated by successive Wei rulers at the instigation of the rival Taoists, sometimes interfered with the work, and most extant examples of sculpture from Yün-kang postdate the destructive Buddhist persecutions which took place from A.D. 444-452. The rock-cut cave-temples at Yün-kang have, however, yielded a vast amount of Buddhist sculpture, largely from the fifth century although some are of later date. They represent a unique and very important body of material for the study of early Chinese sculpture.

In A.D. 494 the Wei capital was moved south to Lo-yang, and a new and even more ambitious group of cave-temples was hollowed out at Lung-mên ('Dragon Gate'), a few miles outside the new capital. The work at Lung-mên was carried out over a period of several centuries, continuing through the T'ang Dynasty, but the best work was produced during two periods: the late fifth and first half of the sixth centuries under the Wei Dynasty and in the seventh and first half of the eighth centuries under the T'ang Dynasty. Work was also carried out at other sites, notably at Hsiang-t'ang Shan, Honan, during the Northern Ch'i Dynasty (Pl. 46), and at T'ien-lung Shan, Shansi. Some of the work at the latter site is of Northern Ch'i date, but the most important work was done during the seventh and early eighth centuries. The T'ang sculpture from T'ien-lung Shan is notable for its strong Indian influence, shown by a more sensuous treatment of the bodies and a fuller realization of the plastic qualities of sculpture. The sandstone figure of a Bodhisattva, standing in a relaxed pose and with flowing scarves falling over the semi-nude body, is a particularly fine example of the T'ien lung Shan style (Pl. 48).

The carving and setting up of votive steles was another important form of Buddhist sculpture. Quite a few such steles are known from the Six Dynasties and T'ang periods, when Buddhism was at its greatest height, and typical examples can be seen in a number of collections. The carving and dedication of such a monument, sometimes involving large numbers of donors and hundreds of workmen, was considered an act of merit, destined to ensure the salvation of all those involved in the enterprise. The museum is indeed fortunate to have in its collection a very fine Northern Wei stele, from southern Shansi or Shensi, dated to A.D. 523 by inscription (Pl. 45). Rows of donors are depicted on the back of the monument, and there are also several donor niches below the principal Buddhist group on the face of the stele.

# Chinese Ceramics

The collection also includes a very important white marble Buddha of Northern Ch'i date (A.D. 577), particularly significant because it shows a curious combination of Chinese and Indian elements (Pl. 47). The parallel, crescent-shaped folds across the front of the body seem to have been derived from the style of the Mathurā school in India. The thin drapery and suggestion of slight modelling of the body underneath also suggest Indian prototypes, but the general massiveness, solidity and static symmetry of the figure are in keeping with Chinese ideals.

A number of important Buddhist sculptures of wood made in the centuries following the fall of the T'ang Dynasty, when wood came to replace the use of stone as a medium for sculpture, round out the collection. Particularly noteworthy are the two dated Bodhisattvas, Kuan-yin and Ta-shi-chih, bearing a Chin Dynasty date corresponding to A.D. 1195 (colour, p. 61; Pl. 75). The two figures, with gently swaying bodies and flowing scarves, seem remarkably similar in style to the two standing Bodhisattvas in the foreground of the large Maitreya fresco, painted only slightly more than a hundred years later (frontispiece, Pl. 2).

The collection of Chinese ceramics covers virtually the entire span from the prehistoric period to the end of the nineteenth century. Most of the major wares are represented, and show the progress and development of ceramic techniques and types from examples of Painted Pottery of about 2500 B.C. to beautifully finished porcelains of the Ch'ing Dynasty (A.D. 1644-1912), decorated in underglaze blue (Pl. 93) or with high-fired enamels applied over the glaze (Pl. 96).

The examples of neolithic Painted Pottery from Kansu, although few in number, are representative of the designs and bold shapes which characterize this ware (Pl. 14,15). The more extensive group of Shang and Chou pottery, much of it of the Gray or Black Pottery type, often complements the collection of ritual bronzes of this era, in both shapes and decorative motifs used to embellish the vessels. Much more unusual, however, is the glazed stoneware jar from An-yang (Pl. 8), perhaps a forerunner of Han Dynasty Proto-Porcelain (Pl. 38, 39).

With the establishment of the Han Dynasty in 206 B.C., China came to enjoy the benefits deriving from a strong centralized empire which, except for a brief interregnum (A.D. 9-23), was to last for almost four hundred years. During this time the custom of burying with the dead pottery models and replicas of the material possessions treasured during life became widespread, and the collection is fortunate in having an unusually rich representation of Han funerary wares. These include various types of pottery wine jars (Pl. 40), their shapes often paralleling those of the Late Chou and Han Dynasty bronze *hu*, storage jars, models of watchtowers (Pl. 12), houses, cooking vessels and stoves, granary urns, wellheads, chicken coops, pigpens and fish ponds, as well as models of various domestic animals. In other words, virtually all aspects of the material culture of Han civilization were reproduced in pottery, to be deposited in the tomb of the deceased. Han funerary wares thus provide an invaluable record of the period.

The most commonly found Han ware is a reddish, sometimes gray earthenware, covered with a low-fired green lead-silicate glaze (Pl. 12, 40, 41). In most cases the glaze has taken on a silvery iridescence as a result of burial. Such iridescence is very often a distinguishing mark of Han pottery. An important aspect of Han burial objects is represented by pottery tomb figures, a very fine example of which is illustrated here (Pl. 42). It is generally assumed that the practice of making

**8** JAR
*Shang Dynasty, An-yang period, c. 1300-1028 B.C. From An-yang, Honan.*
*Glazed stoneware  H. 8 5/16 in. (21.1 cm.)  Dr. James M. Menzies Collection, 960.238.35*

Hard-fired ceramics with glaze were uncovered in excavations at An-yang, site of the capital during the latter part of the Shang dynasty. They are the first evidence of what may be a predecessor to true porcelain, developed in China more than a thousand years later. These early wares indicate that the technical skill of the Chinese potter was already greatly advanced and that it was possible for the Shang potters to attain very high temperatures in their kilns.

PUBL.: B. Stephen, 'Some Chinese Archaeological Discoveries in the Menzies Collection,' *Annual, R.O.M.,* 1962, pp. 59-60 and Pl. XXV; T. A. Heinrich, *Art Treasures in the Royal Ontario Museum,* Toronto, 1963, p. 30.

tomb figures of pottery, or of wood, such as the Late Chou example from Ch'ang-sha in Hunan Province (Pl. 7), replaced the earlier Shang practice of human sacrifice associated with the burial of an important person. Making pottery models of human figures to accompany the deceased into the nether world was continued well into the Ming Dynasty, as shown by the many tomb figures from this period. The Museum has a remarkable group of Wei figures, dating from the early sixth century, which illustrate certain refinements of style when compared to earlier Han examples (Pl. 43). The Wei figures show a keen observation of dress and personal ornament, and a distinct effort to express the individual character and ethnic features of the personages portrayed. The slightly later group of figures, three of which are illustrated in the Handbook, in foreign dress and distinguished by non-Chinese features, may suggest the possible influence of the Buddhist art of Central Asia (Pl. 44).

The collection's extensive holdings of T'ang and Sung ceramics illustrate remarkably well the full development of Chinese ceramic art. In the T'ang Dynasty, a period remembered not only for the splendour and glories of the empire but also for its great artistic achievements, the green lead glaze typical of many of the Han wares gave way to the use of bright polychrome glazes, often mottled and streaked. Combinations of three or more colours, particularly green, a straw-coloured yellow, amber and blue, are common and have given rise to the term "three-colour" glaze. The same colours also occur as monochromes. The bright T'ang glazes were still of the lead-silicate group, corresponding to the popular Han glaze. They were applied over a pottery body, and were fired at low temperatures. White wares represent another important group of T'ang ceramics. The white wares are frequently of pottery or stoneware to which a translucent glaze has been applied over a white slip (Pl. 58, 59), but thin, translucent porcelain is sometimes encountered. The beautiful stem cup (Pl. 56) is an outstanding example of T'ang porcelain. It also provides important evidence of the manufacture of pure porcelain as early as the T'ang Dynasty.

Sung ceramics (A.D. 960-1279) are often regarded as the highest achievements of the Chinese potter. They correspond to the advanced and sophisticated state of Sung civilization, and show a sharp departure from their predecessors in taste and technique. The Sung wares favour vitrified monochrome glazes fired at high temperatures, and true porcelain or por-

18

cellaneous stoneware bodies. They show a preference for elegant, refined shapes rather than the bolder, more vigorous T'ang shapes and polychrome glazes which reflect the adventurous, military spirit of the earlier age. Iron and copper were the principal colouring agents of the feldspathic Sung glazes, clearly foreshadowing the ceramic art of the Ming and Ch'ing periods and the final achievements of Chinese porcelain manufacture.

Many of the most important types of Sung ceramics are represented in the collection. They range from the elegant yet simple Tz'u-chou wares, decorated in a variety of techniques employing a combination of cream-coloured or other slips, brown and black glazes, and incised, carved or cut-away designs (Pl. 66, 67), to the monochrome wares of Ting (Pl. 71, 72), Chien (Pl. 73), Celadon (Pl. 70) and other types.

With the possible exception of the group of Ming and Transitional blue-and-white porcelains, the Museum's holdings of Ming (A.D. 1368-1644) and Ch'ing (A.D. 1644-1912) porcelains cannot at present match in either extent or scope the collection's T'ang and Sung ceramics. The technique of decorating porcelain with designs painted in cobalt blue under a transparent white glaze had already been practised in the Yüan Dynasty and possibly earlier, but in the Ming period blue-and-white porcelain came into great demand and rose to its highest achievements (Pl. 83-86). Many of the Ming porcelains were made for the Emperor and court, but large numbers were exported to other parts of Asia, the Near East and Europe. In the Ming and Transitional periods, decoration in underglaze blue, sometimes (especially in the sixteenth century) with the addition of overglaze enamels, continued to be a favourite technique. In the Ch'ing Dynasty the enamelling technique, whereby vitrifiable enamels would be applied over a white porcelain glaze, replaced blue-and-white porcelain in importance, even though the latter was still produced in large numbers. The green or *famille verte* enamels are characteristic of the K'ang-hsi reign (A.D. 1622-1772), but the addition of a rose-coloured enamel, the *famille rose* technique, was introduced in the Yung-chêng reign (A.D. 1723-1735) and continued in use through the Ch'ien-lung period (A.D. 1736-1795).

Not all the many and varied types of Ming and Ch'ing porcelains are represented in the collection, but the fine K'ang-hsi vase, with decoration in underglaze blue and *tou-ts'ai* enamels (Pl. 96), is a very good example of the enamelling technique. On the other hand, the seated figure of Wên Ch'ang Ti Chün, Patron God of Literature, of fine Tê-hua porcelain with a grayish white glaze, illustrates an important aspect of Ch'ing monochrome porcelain (Pl. 95).

# Chinese Lacquer

Our knowledge concerning the beginnings of lacquer manufacture in China is still very incomplete, but we are on firmer ground when we reach the Late Chou period (c. 600-222 B.C.). Examples of lacquer, often in the form of shallow bowls or 'eared cups' (yu-shang), have been found at Ch'ang-sha and other Late Chou sites. An oval cup in the collection with two projecting flanges is typical of the yu-shang type. Han lacquer is even better known from excavations at Ch'ang-sha, at Lo-lang, in Korea, and at sites in Outer Mongolia, but we know little of later lacquers prior to the Yüan Dynasty. As the manufacture of ceramics developed, expecially in the T'ang Dynasty, the production of lacquer vessels undoubtedly declined. Beginning, however, with the Yüan Dynasty (A.D. 1280-1368), new lacquer techniques were again invented and in the Ming Dynasty lacquer was in such great demand that many new techniques and styles were introduced.

The lacquer used in China and Japan was obtained from the sap of the lac tree (Rhus vernicifera), which grows over wide areas of China today and was probably even more abundant in earlier times. The sap was carefully purified and strained to produce a viscous, clear liquid which could be applied with a brush and coloured by the addition of various mineral and vegetable dyes. The use of lacquer remained popular throughout the Ming and Ch'ing Dynasties. Lacquer was also popular in Japan, where it was used in a great variety of techniques. It is likely that the lacquer tree was introduced to Japan via Korea about the sixth century.

Three Ming lacquers are illustrated in the Handbook, of which the rarest and most important example is surely the large Cylindrical Box (Pl. 89). No exact parallel to its shape is known, although the design and technique of the carving clearly establish the date of the box to be the early fifteenth century. It is an outstanding and exceptionally fine example of early Ming carved lacquer. In this technique a layer of hempen, silk or silken fabric and a paste of clay and varnish were ordinarily used to cover the wood core before the application of the lacquer. The base was then built up by successive layers of lacquer, perhaps as many as fifty, before the design was carved.

Other Ming lacquers in the collection illustrate the variety of techniques available to the lacquer craftsmen. The beautifully carved Box (Pl. 92) and a recently acquired Tray of the sixteenth century serve as fine illustrations of the guri technique, in which alternate layers of black and red were applied.

9  HEXAGONAL DISH
*Ming Dynasty, six-character Chia-ching mark and period (1522-66)*
*Lacquer  H. 1 1/2 in. (3.8 cm.); w. 7 1/2 in. (19 cm.)  961.201.2*

Multi-coloured lacquer with successive layers of red, green and buff-brown. Carved decoration of Taoist subjects. In centre, flower basket supported on large lotus above motif of rocks and waves. Stylized *shou* (longevity) character and two trigrams above. Cavetto decorated with six panels with alternate designs of five-clawed dragons and cranes amid clouds. On exterior, six panels with peach and fungus sprays above narrow key-fret band round foot. Chia-ching mark carved through red lacquer of base and filled with gold.

PUBL.: H. Trubner, 'Ming Lacquer in the Royal Ontario Museum,' *Annual*, ROM, 1962, Pl. XVIII.

The Hexagonal Dish (Pl. 9) with the Chia-ching reign mark is an excellent example of Ming multi-coloured lacquer, in which layers of red, green, and buff-brown lacquer were superimposed in successive applications.

# Chinese Painting

Chinese painting was already flourishing in the last centuries before the Christian era, and developed into an important form of artistic expression during the Han Dynasty (206 B.C. – A.D. 220). In this period, painting generally took the form of wall paintings. Suggestions of this type of decoration are reflected in some of the designs on secondary Han material, such as tomb tiles with mould-pressed designs, stone reliefs, ceramics with moulded designs, and other objects (Pl. 4, 35-37, 40, 41). Hunting scenes and mythological subjects were among the favourite themes found on these objects.

The development of figure painting and of landscape during the Six Dynasties and T'ang periods cannot be shown here for lack of material, nor is painting of the Sung Dynasty, perhaps the greatest age of Chinese painting, represented. Fortunately the collection's lack of Six Dynasties, T'ang and Sung paintings is compensated, at least in part, by the presence of a group of three Yüan Dynasty wall paintings. The best and earliest example, from the beginning of the fourteenth century, represents Maitreya Buddha enthroned in the centre, accompanied by Bodhisattvas and a host of other divine beings (Pl. 2). It was originally set up in the Northern Hall of the Hsiang-hua-ssu ('Monastery of Joyful Conversion') in southeast Shansi. Although somewhat earlier, it is similar in style to another well-known group of Buddhist wall paintings from the same general area in Shansi, presently installed in the University Museum, Philadelphia (a pair of frescoes), the Nelson Gallery, Kansas City, and in the Metropolitan Museum of Art, New York. Buddhist painting, particularly in the form of large frescoes, had been perfected during the T'ang Dynasty; the monumental Maitreya group in the ROM collection still reflects the powerful T'ang style in the sweeping composition and vigorous brushwork.

Landscape painting, which rose to a brilliant development in the tenth century, continued to be the dominant and perhaps most noble form of Chinese pictorial art during the Sung and subsequent periods. The crisp yet powerful ink style of the landscape painters active in the tenth century gradually gave way, in the Sung Dynasty, to a richer, more impressionistic treatment of landscape, as exemplified by such thirteenth century masters as Ma Yüan and Hsia Kuei. Ultimately, in the Ming Dynasty, many different schools flourished side by side, principally centred around the Wu school, the 'literati' or scholar-painters, and the Chê school (from the old name of the Chêkiang region), represented by the conservative academicians and official court painters. T'ang Yin, the master of the hanging scroll 'Scholar in a Summer Landscape' (Pl. 10), is representative of the academic Chê school. The dynamic composition of soaring peaks ultimately derives from the Northern Sung landscape style, particularly as represented by the work of Li T'ang (fl. c. 1100-1130). But the Ming version is more unilateral, with a strong movement towards the left and greater emphasis on diagonal thrusts and jagged peaks, combined with a powerful depiction of contorted trees, their roots twisted and exposed, and massive, piled-up rocks. Compared to its Sung predecessors, the painting shows a greater sense of angular movement, solidity of the forms, and intensity of expression. The scroll not only exemplifies T'ang Yin's skill as a painter, but also illustrates some of the fundamental aspects of Ming painting, as expressed by the more conservative Chê school.

山銀決決路迢迢惆悵閒
行過野橋繩樹一林斜
日裏飄些巾影倩誰
橫吳楊唐寅為
成嵩宋君畫

**10** 'SCHOLAR IN A SUMMER LANDSCAPE'
*By T'ang Yin (1470-1523)    Ming Dynasty*
*Hanging scroll in ink and slight colour on satin silk    H. 53 1/2 in.*
*(135.9 cm.); w. 21 3/8 in. (54.3 cm.)    957.19*

Poem by T'ang Yin in upper right. Three seals of painter and numerous collectors' seals, including ten seals of Hsiang Yüan-pien (1525-
90), famous Ming collector, calligrapher and connoisseur.
T'ang Yin was a native of Su-chou, centre of the Wu school. Artisti-
cally and socially he stands mid-way between the conservative
academicians of the Chê school and the scholar-painters of the more
progressive Wu school. His successful career as a public official was
unfortunately marred by his involvement in an examination scandal.
T'ang Yin felt disgraced and turned to the carefree life of a Bohemian,
taking to wine and enjoying the pleasure quarters of Su-chou.

PUBL.: S. E. Lee, *Chinese Landscape Painting*, Cleveland Museum of
Art, 1954, No. 47; *Loan Exhibition of Chinese Paintings*, organized
by Frank Caro, selection and text by Hsien-ch'i Tsêng, Royal Ontario
Museum, 1956, No. 18; H. Trubner, 'A Painting by T'ang Yin,' *Annual*,
ROM, 1959, pp. 46-49; *1000 Jahre Chinesische Malerei*, Haus der Kunst,
Munich, 1960, No. 46; T. A. Heinrich, *Art Treasures in the Royal
Ontario Museum*, Toronto, 1963, p. 64.

11 CEREMONIAL VESSEL (*yu*)
*Shang Dynasty, An-yang period, c. 1300-1028 B.C.*
*Bronze H. 13 3/4 in. (34.9 cm.) Purchased with funds from the*
*Reuben Wells Leonard Bequest, 954.136.5*

Decorated with narrow band with 'dissolved' *t'ao-t'ieh* around the
neck and cover, a third decorative band around the foot. The handle,
decorated with chevron pattern on *lei-wên* ground, terminates in two
bovine heads with spiral horns.
Although the exact purpose of many of the vessels is not known,
their function can often be deduced from ancient records. The *yu*
was intended as a wine container and, like most of the vessels, was
probably used in ceremonies connected with ancestor worship. This
*yu*, with restrained bands of decoration of the type used in late
Shang and early Chou, retains the tall form characteristic of earlier
Shang examples.

CF. S. Umehara, *Nihon Shūcho Shina Kodō Seikwa*, Vol. 1, Osaka,
1959, Pl. XLIX, *yu* in Neiraku Art Museum, Nara.

PUBL.: H. E. Fernald, 'Six Bronze Vessels from China,' *R.O.M.A.
Bulletin*, No. 23, May, 1955, Fig. 4.

12 MODEL OF A WATCHTOWER
*Later Han Dynasty, A.D. 25-221*
*Pottery with iridescent green glaze H. 47 in. (1 m., 20 cm.); dia.
of moat 14 1/2 in. (36.7 cm.) 925.25.7*

This funerary model of a watchtower is reported to have come from
Lo-yang. The architecture consists of a square tower with three
principal stories, balconies, latticed windows and overhanging, tiled
roofs. Complex three-armed brackets support the eaves and individual
stories. Supports in the form of bears are mounted at the four corners
beneath the two balconies. The tower is surrounded by a moat with
two horses and riders mounted on the rim. Other figures are placed
on the balustrades of the tower.

PUBL.: H. Trubner, *Arts of the Han Dynasty*, Chinese Art Society of
America, Asia House, New York, 1961, No. 7 (*frontispiece*); *Archives*,
Vol. XIV, 1960, p. 2; T. A. Heinrich, *Art Treasures in the Royal
Ontario Museum*, Toronto, 1963, pp. 34-35.

13 BOWL
*Chin Dynasty, 13th century*
*Tz'u-chou ware   Dia. 6 1/16 in. (15.4 cm.)   918.21.394*

Lotus design in overglaze red, green and yellow enamels. Transparent glaze over white slip. The use of overglaze enamels was an important technical innovation of the Tz'u-chou potters. It led to the technique of decorating porcelain in high-fired enamels, often in combination with painted designs in underglaze blue, a technique perfected during the Ming and early part of the Ch'ing period.

PUBL.: T. A. Heinrich, *Art Treasures in the Royal Ontario Museum,* Toronto, 1963, p. 59.

**14** JAR
*Kansu type, Yang-shao neolithic, Pan-shan stage, c. 2000 B.C.*
*Painted pottery   H. 14 7/8 in. (37.7 cm.)   930.20.4*

Reddish pottery with geometric decoration in red and black. Large globular jars of this type, with painted decoration, are characteristic of the mortuary ceramics found in graves of the neolithic Yang-shao culture at Pan-shan, in Kansu. These finely-made ceramics seem to have been reserved almost exclusively for burials, while plain, rather rough wares were used for everyday purposes.

CF. Nils Palmgren, 'Kansu Mortuary Urns of the Pan Shan and Ma Chang Groups,' *Palaeonotologia Sinica*, Series D, Vol. III, Part 1, Peking, 1934, Pls. XV, XVI.

**15** JAR
*Kansu type, Yang-shao neolithic, Pan-shan stage, c. 2000 B.C.*
*Painted pottery   H. 9 1/8 in. (23.1 cm.)   930.20.1*

Reddish brown pottery with geometric decoration in red and black, and two snakes modelled in relief on opposite sides of body. Pottery funerary wares with painted decoration, found in many areas of North China, generally represent an earlier stage than the black and gray potteries. Since these painted wares resemble pottery found far to the west of China, they have sometimes been cited as possible evidence of an intrusive culture of western origin.

PUBL.: 'West-East,' *R.O.M.A. Bulletin*, No. 21, Oct., 1953, No. 40; T. A. Heinrich, *Art Treasures in the Royal Ontario Museum*, Toronto, 1963, p. 30.

17 CEREMONIAL VESSEL *(ting)*
*Shang Dynasty, An-yang period, c. 1300-1028 B.C.*
*Bronze H. 13 3/8 in. (33.9 cm.) Purchased with funds from the Reuben Wells Leonard Bequest, 954.136.1*

The body of this tripod is covered with a geometric design of inter-locked T's on a ground of *lei-wên* or 'thunder pattern' spiral ground, similar to the decoration on some of the carved, white pottery of the Shang dynasty. The combination of angular surface decoration with subtly curving form is also characteristic of the Shang style.

PUBL.: P. Ackerman, *Ritual Bronzes of Ancient China*, New York, 1945, Pl. 15; Saturday Night, December 11, 1954; H. E. Fernald, 'Six Bronze Vessels from China,' *R.O.M.A. Bulletin*, No. 23, May, 1955, Fig. 2; T. A. Heinrich, *Art Treasures in the Royal Ontario Museum*, Toronto, 1963, p. 31.

16 CEREMONIAL VESSEL *(hu)*
*Shang Dynasty, An-yang period, c. 1300-1028 B.C.*
*Bronze H. 15 3/8 in. (39 cm.) Purchased with funds from the Reuben Wells Leonard Bequest, 945.136.3*

Decoration in horizontal bands, with *t'ao-t'ieh* masks, birds and dragons against *lei-wên* or 'thunder pattern' spiral ground. The *t'ao-t'ieh* mask with its bulging eyes is the most distinctive motif employed by the early Chinese artist. Its significance is unknown but the frequency of its appearance indicates that it must have had some important meaning. Always organized around prominent eyes, a single mask often contains stylized elements suggesting a number of different animal species, though horns or other features usually give a general bovine or feline character. The *lei-wên* pattern, of round or square spirals, was regarded as a symbol of thunder and lightning.

PUBL.: H. E. Fernald, 'Six Bronze Vessels from China,' *R.O.M.A. Bulletin*, No. 23, May, 1955, Fig. 3; T. A. Heinrich, *Art Treasures in the Royal Ontario Museum*, Toronto, 1963, p. 31.

26

**19** SQUARE MIRROR
*Late Chou Dynasty, c. 500 B.C. Reportedly from Chin-ts'un*
*Bronze inlaid with turquoise  3 9/16 in. (9.1 cm.) x 3 9/16 in.*
*923.16.107*

Square mirror made of two bronze plates soldered together. The reflecting plate, slightly smaller, is secured to a larger upper part, decorated with an openwork design of two pairs of phoenix-like birds, their heads turned back to back, their necks touching in the centre. A pair of inverted, heart-shaped ornaments placed between the breasts of the confronted birds is apparently a prototype of a similar motif on Karlgren's type C (Shou-chou type) mirror. A lyre-shaped motif occupies the space between the back and wings on each pair of birds. The back and wing feathers have a stylized scale pattern, also found on Late Chou bronze vessels. The lower bodies are covered with a striated pattern of lines. A triangular meander design of finely incised lines forms the border of the mirror. There are remains of turquoise inlay in the heart and lyre-shaped motifs.
The primitive technique of casting two separate plates, as well as the square shape itself, confirm the dating of the mirror in the Late Chou period, when mirrors were not primarily practical but symbolic and magical objects. It is one of the finest examples of this early type.

CF. S. Umehara, *Kan Izen no Kokyō no Kenkyū*, Koyoto, 1935, pl. 35, Fig. 1, and p. 37, Fig. 20.

PUBL.: W. C. White, *Tombs of Old Lo-yang*, Shanghai, 1934, Pl. LI, No. 128; S. Umehara, Kan Izen no Kokyō no Kenkyū (L'étude sur le miroir anterieur à la Dynastie des 'Han'), Kyoto, 1935, Fig. 2, No. 7; Rakuyō Kinson Kobo Shūei, Kyoto, 1937, Pl. L; A. Salmony, 'On Early Chinese Mirrors,' *Art in America*, Vol. 30, 1942, p. 196, Fig. 5; 'The Art of Eastern Chou,' *Chinese Art Society of America*, 1962, No. 57; Emmy Bunker, 'A Little Known Type of Eastern Han Mirror,' *Archives*, Vol. XVII, 1963, p. 40, Fig. 5; D. Dohrenwend, 'The Early Chinese Mirror,' *Artibus Asiae*, Vol. XXVII, Nos. 1/2, 1964, Pl. I, Fig. 1D.

**18** CEREMONIAL VESSEL *(chih)*
*Shang Dynasty, An-yang period, c. 1300-1028 B.C.*
*Bronze  H. 7 3/4 in. (19.65 cm.)  Lee of Fareham Collection, permanent loan from the Massey Foundation, L.960.9.123*

The owl has a prominent place in Shang art, lending its form to a variety of bronze vessels. Here it decorates a small bronze wine cup with cover. Like many of the *t'ao-t'ieh* masks, the owl's body has been spread so that it envelops the vessel. It may be viewed from each side, either as two confronted birds in profile or as one bird seen full face. It is set against a ground of small, square spirals of the *lei-wên* type.

CF. S. Mizuno, *Bronzes and Jades of Ancient China*, Tokyo, 1959, Pl. 39.

**20 SQUARE VESSEL**

*Late Chou Dynasty, Warring States period, 480-222 B.C. Reportedly from Chin-ts'un, near Lo-yang, Honan*
*Bronze H. 7 13/16 in. (19.8 cm.); l. and w., 11 15/16 in. (30.3 cm.) x 11 15/16 in. Bishop White Collection, 933.12.54*

The custom of inlaying bronze with other materials, first seen in Shang times, was revived during the latter part of the Chou dynasty. The vessel has an inlaid geometric design in gold, copper and turquoise round the exterior of the rim. The fine relief design of spirals on the body, and the interlaced openwork of the cover, in the form of entwined snakes, are also characteristic of the finest bronze work of this period. There is some question whether the cover actually belongs to this vessel, although there is no doubt that it is from the same period.

PUBL.: *Illustrated London News*, October 28, 1933, p. 701, Fig. 7; W. C. White, *Tombs of Old Lo-yang*, Shanghai, 1934, Pl. CXIII; J. G. Anderson, 'The Goldsmith in Ancient China,' *B.M.F.E.A.*, Vol. 7, 1934, Pls. II-IH; S. Umehara, *Rakuyō Kinson Kobo Shūei*, Kyoto, 1937, App., Pl. VII; B. Karlgren, 'Huai and Han,' *B.M.F.E.A.*, Vol. 13, 1941, Pl. 6, Fig. 6; L. Bachhofer, *A Short History of Chinese Art*, London, 1946, p. 47, Fig. XII.

21  OVAL VESSEL WITH COVER *(ting)*
*Late Chou Dynasty, Warring States period, 480-222 B.C. Reportedly from Chin-ts'un*
*Bronze   H. 5 1/8 in. (12.85 cm.); l. 7 7/8 in. (20 cm.)   Bishop White Collection, 932.16.71*

Decoration confined to portions which project from body; oval grip which tops lid, ring handles with animal heads, and four supporting figures with rings and bird heads. Small details, such as pupils of figures' eyes, inlaid with dark glass.

CF. almost identical vessel in B. Karlgren, *The Pillsbury Collection of Chinese Bronzes*, Minneapolis, 1952, Pl. 70, No. 50.

PUBL.: *Illustrated London News*, October 28, 1933, p. 701, Fig. 3; W. C. White, *Tombs of Old Lo-yang*, Shanghai, 1934, Frontispiece and Pl. C; S. Umehara, *Rakuyō Kinson Kobo Shūei*, Kyoto, 1937, Pl. VI; *The Art of Eastern Chou*, Chinese Art Society of America, New York, 1962, No. 40.

22  CEREMONIAL VESSEL WITH COVER AND SNAKE SUPPORTS *(tui)*
*Late Chou Dynasty, Warring States period, 480-222 B.C. Reportedly from Chin-ts'un*
*Bronze   H. 7 13/16 in (19.8 cm.); dia. 6 3/32 in. (15.5 cm.)*
*933.12.65*

This vessel is a version of the *ting* tripod as modified during Late Chou. Following a tendency seen earlier to make the lid serviceable as a dish when removed and inverted, this lid is actually the same size and form as the body, even to the snake support which may function either as handles or as legs.

CF. S. Umehara, *Sengoku Shiki Dōki no Kenkyū*, Kyoto, 1936, Pls. XLIII, LXIV, XLVI.

PUBL.: W. C. White, *Tombs of Old Lo-yang*, Shanghai, 1934, Pl. XCIX (other of identical pair); cf. also Pls. XCVII, XCVIII.

**23 KNEELING FIGURE**
*Late Chou Dynasty, Warring States period, 480-222 B.C. Reportedly
from Chin-ts'un*
*Bronze   H. 10 3/8 in. (26 cm.)   929.11.27*

Figure kneeling with crossed feet on small, flat base and holding in
the extended hands a hollow tube above cylindrical socket, the latter
presumably supporting originally a staff or architectural part. The
face, with round, big eyes, thick lips and broad face, realistically
modelled, does not represent characteristic Chinese features, but
rather a type of face associated with nomads of Central Asia. The tight
costume with short sleeves, and the left lapel overlapping the right,
suggests a hunting costume worn by Scythians, which is different
from the loose-fitting Chinese costume. Of particular interest is the
belt hook, of Scythian derivation, and one of the earliest representations of the belt hook in Chinese art. The head is covered by a type
of 'openwork helmet,' broad at the back and raised at the top, then
narrowing towards the forehead, while the sides of the head are left
uncovered. A crossing strap runs down in front of the ears and
below the chin. A second strap runs along the top of the forehead,
above the ears and around the back of the head.
The figure is believed to be one of a pair, the companion piece being in
the Minneapolis Institute of Arts. Both figures are bronze *ming-ch'i*,
objects intended for the service of the souls in the spirit world.

CF. *C. T. Loo Catalogue*, 1941, No. 72 (Pillsbury Coll.); O. R. T. Jansé,
*Archaeological Research in Indo China*, Vol. 1, Harvard-Yenching
Institute Monograph Series, Vol. VII, Cambridge, 1947, Pl. 55; Figs.
8-12; B. Karlgren, *A Catalogue of the Chinese Bronzes in the Alfred
F. Pillsbury Collection*, Minneapolis, 1952, No. 96, Pls. 110-111; L.
Sickman and A. Soper, *The Art and Architecture of China*, Harm-
ondsworth, 1956, Pl. 8 C (Pillsbury Coll.); *Handbook, Nelson Gallery
of Art*, Kansas City, 1959, p. 174; Daisy Lion Goldschmidt, *Chinese
Art*, tr. by Jean-Claude Moreau-Gobard, New York, 1960, Pl. 94 (Coll.
of Mme. Pinket, Brussels); S. Pigott, *Dawn of Civilization*, London,
1961, p. 261 (Pillsbury Coll.); *The Art of the Eastern Chou*, Chinese
Art Society of America, New York, 1962, (Nelson Gallery, Kansas
City); Chêng Te-k'un, *Chou China*, Cambridge, 1963, Pl. 30 a.

PUBL.: J. C. Ferguson, 'Bronze Figures,' *China Journal*, Vol. XIV, 1931,
No. 4, facing p. 162; A. Salmony, *Sino-Siberian Art in the Collection
of C. T. Loo*, Paris, 1933, Pl. XVIII, No. 3; W. C. White, *Tombs of Old
Lo-yang*, Shanghai, 1934 Pl. LXXVIII; S. Umehara, "Sengoku Shiki Dōki
no Kenkyū (A Study of Bronzes of the Warring States Period),' Tōhō
Bunka Gakuin Kyoto Kenkyūjo, *Kenkyū Hōkoku*, Vol. 7, Kyoto,
1936, p. 67, Fig. 22; S. Mizuno, 'Chōsa shutsudo no Mokugu ni tsuite,'
*Tōhō Gakuhō*, Kyoto, 1937, p. 234, Fig. 5; Rakuyō Kinson Kobo Shūei,
Kyoto, 1937, p. 33; L. Bachhofer, 'Bronze Figures of the Late Chou
Period,' *Art Bulletin*, Vol. XXII, No. 4, 1941, pp. 317-331, Figs. 1-2; T.
Nagahiro, 'Obikoma no Kenkyū (A Study on Belthooks),' *Tōhō
Bunka Kenkyūjo Hōkoku*, Vol. 17, Kyoto, 1943, p. 82, Fig. 28; L.
Bachhofer, *A Short History of Chinese Art*, London, 1946, Pl. 52;
*Sekai Kōkogaku Taikei*, Vol. 6, Tokyo, 1958, p. 95, Pls. 223, 225.

30

**24 HANDLE**
*Late Chou Dynasty, 5th – 3rd Century* B.C. *Reportedly from Chints'un.*
*Bronze with gold and silver inlay H. 2 23/32 in. (6.19 cm.); w. 3 5/16 in. (8.4 cm.)* 931.13.74

Inlay of gold and silver wires in spiral and volute pattern, characteristic of objects from Lo-yang. Handle has a rather flat, slender, hollow bar connecting the two ends. Hole for fastening at base of one end. Because of their flat shape, handles of this type are believed to have been used horizontally, rather than vertically.
Cf. S. Umehara, *Rakuyō Kinson Kobo Shūei*, Kyoto, 1937, Pl. LXV and pp. 38-39.

PUBL.: W. C. White, *Tombs of Old Lo-yang*, Shanghai, 1934, Pl. V, No. 007 b

**25 ANIMAL HEAD FINIALS**
*Late Chou Dynasty, 5th – 3rd century* B.C. *Reportedly from Chints'un.*
*Bronze with gold and silver inlay* H. (931.13.70) 2 15/16 in. (7.4 cm.); w. 2 in. (5 cm.)  H. (931.13.71) 2 7/8 in. (7.3 cm.); w. 2 1/6 in. (5.2 cm.)

Elegant bronze finials in the form of stylized reptilian heads in full relief, presumably part of the chariot ornament. The socketed ends, containing fragments of wood, had been attached by means of bronze pins. The features are defined by fine gold and silver wires in spiral and volute pattern, emphasizing especially the tusks and eyes. The inlaid designs were executed by placing a number of narrow metal threads (1/3 mm. wide) side by side and then hammering them together into the desired shape. The designs on these two heads differ slightly, suggesting that they form part of different pairs.

CF. Handbook, Nelson Gallery of Art – Atkins Museum, Kansas City, 1959, p. 175; S. Umehara, *Rakuyō Kinson Kobo Shūei*, Kyoto, pl. LXIII.

PUBL.: W. C. White, *Tombs of Old Lo-yang*, Shanghai, 1934, Pl. VI, No. 015 a – b, Pl. VII (line drawing); *The Art of Eastern Chou*, Chinese Art Society of America, New York, 1962, No. 35.

**26 PAIR OF FINIALS**
*Late Chou Dynasty, 5th – 3rd century* B.C. *Reportedly from Chints'un*
*Bronze with gold and silver inlay  L. 2 9/16 in. (6.5 cm.); dia. (at base) 1 1/4 in. (3.2 cm.)* 929.11.78, 929.11.140

Pair of small, cylindrical bronze finials with inlay of gold and silver wires in conventional style of Late Chou covering body; capped ends with circular and geometric design. Holes near base used for fastening to wooden shaft.

PUBL.: W. C. White, *Tombs of Old Lo-yang*, Shanghai, 1934, Pl. LV, No. 011 a and b; Pl. VII, No. 011 (line drawing).

**28 PENDANT**
*Late Chou Dynasty, 5th – 3rd century B.C.  Reportedly from Chin-ts'un*
*Brown and green jade  H. 1 9/16 in. (3.9 cm.); l. 5 in. (12.7 cm.)*
931.13.16

Pendant in form of double-headed dragon. Design of small scrolls in relief on both sides of entire body, the wings and tail treated with lines. The detailed and precise carving of this and other jades illustrated reflects the high technical accomplishment and superb craftsmanship attained in the Late Chou period.

PUBL.: W. C. White, *Tombs of Old Lo-yang*, Shanghai, 1934, Pl. CXXVI, No. 313 b.

**27 PAIR OF FINIALS**
*Late Chou Dynasty, 5th – 3rd century B.C.  Reportedly from Chin-ts'un*
*Bronze with gold and silver inlay  L. (931.13.9) 4 3/32 in. (10.4 cm.); dia. (at base) 1 3/8 in. (3.5 cm.)  L. (931.13.130) 4 1/8 in. (10.5 cm.); dia. (at base) 1 3/8 in. (3.5 cm.)*

Pair of baluster-shaped bronze finials with inlay of gold and silver wires in spiral and volute pattern, as well as lozenge-shaped designs, alternating with hanging blade motif. On top, circular glass disc with moulded rib and revolving 'eye' design of pearl shape, characteristic of glass beads and small glass inlays obtained from tombs of the Eastern Chou period.

CF. S. Umehara, *Rakuyō Kinson Kobo Shūei*, Kyoto, 1937, Pl. LXIII, and p. 37.

PUBL.: W. C. White, *Tombs of Old Lo-yang*, Shanghai, 1934, Pl. VI, No. 014 a – b; 'West-East,' *R.O.M.A. Bulletin*, No. 21, Oct., 1953, No. 71.

**29 PENDANT**
*Late Chou Dynasty, 5th – 3rd century B.C.  Reportedly from Chin-ts'un*
*Yellowish jade  H. 1 3/8 in. (3.5 cm.); l. 3 17/32 in. (9 cm.)*
931.13.17

Pendant of yellowish jade, translucent in middle and turning into opaque chocolate brown at edges. Dragon with large crested head turned backward, fish-like tail and arched back which has small hole for suspension. Entire body covered on both sides with small scrolls and scale-like design, rendered in finely incised lines.

PUBL.: W. C. White, *Tombs of Old Lo-yang*, Shanghai, 1934, Pl. CXXVII, No. 313 a.

**30 PLAQUE**
*Late Chou Dynasty, 5th – 3rd century* B.C. *Reportedly from Chin-ts'un*
*Dark green jade  H. 1 3/8 in. (3.1 cm.); l. 2 1/4 in. (5.6 cm.)*
*931.13.18*

Plaque in the form of crouching monster with short tail and prominent claws. Finely incised scrolls and cross-hatching, of slightly different design, on the two sides. Small hole at upper centre suggests that the plaque was used as a pendant.

PUBL.: W. C. White, *Tombs of Old Lo-yang*, Shanghai, 1934, Pl. CXXVII, No. 315 a

**31 'HILL' CENSER** *(po-shan-hsiang-lu)*
*Former Han Dynasty, 206* B.C. – A.D. 24
*Bronze  H. 7 1/16 in. (17.9 cm.); dia. (at mouth) 3 1/4 in. (8.2 cm.)*
*922.20.93*

Cover in form of stylized mountain peaks, decorated with human figures and animals in low relief. Scenes of fighting animals reflect the influence of the nomad art of the Ordos region. A design of foliate scrolls covers the underside of the bowl, a wide band of coiled dragons encircles wide part of the foot. A short curved handle, projecting from the side of the bowl, terminates in a feline head.
A possible Ch'ang-sha provenance for the censer is suggested by the very similar design on the cover of a censer from this region illustrated in the catalogue of *An Exhibition of Chinese Antiquities from Ch'ang-sha*, Yale University, 1939, Fig. 8, and A.C. Wenley, "The Question of the Po-shan-hsiang-lu," *Archives*, Vol. III, 1948-49, Pl. II c. Concerning the *po-shan-hsiang-lu*, see also B. Laufer, *Pottery of the Han Dynasty*, Leiden, 1909, pp. 174 ff.

PUBL.: H. Trubner, *Arts of the Han Dynasty*, Chinese Art Society of America, Asia House, New York, 1961, No. 43; *Archives*, Vol. XIV, 1960, p. 34.

**33 PAIR OF MONKEYS**
*Han Dynasty,* 206 B.C. – A.D. 221 *Reportedly from Chin-ts'un*
*Bronze* H. *(930.21.33)* 2 1/8 *in. (5.2 cm.)*
H. *(930.21.34)* 1 15/16 *in. (4.9 cm.)*

The monkeys, both squatting, are rendered in a naturalistic style, foreshadowing some of the later tendencies towards naturalistic representation in the post-Han and T'ang periods. The different sizes and features of the two monkeys suggest that the artist may have attempted to show a male and female monkey. One of them (930.21. 33), perhaps male, has deep wrinkles on the forehead and around the eyes, and large paws, the left on the knee, the right at the mouth. The second monkey, which may be female, has the head turned to the right. It has large, well-shaped eyes, three lines under the neck and a small forehead. The left paw is on the knee, the right rests on the ground.

PUBL.: W. C. White, *Tombs of Old Lo-yang*, Shanghai, 1934, Pl. LXXXV, No. 211 a – b.

**32 CYLINDRICAL VESSEL**
*Han Dynasty,* 206 B.C. – A.D. 221
*Bronze* H. 7 7/16 *in. (19.14 cm.); dia. of lid 5 in. (12.7 cm.)* 932.16.44

Bronze toilet case (*lien*) with lid and handle, supported on three animal-form feet. Cylindrical form, decorated with plain band around the centre and lower part. Cover fits closely over top of vessel and is provided with small rectangular loop in centre. Flattened handle in form of arch with dragon head terminals is attached by means of short chain to two rings which pass through vertical loops on side of box.

CF. Government General of Chōsen, *Museum Exhibits Illustrated*, Vol. L, 1918, Pl. 3; E. A. Voretzsch, *Altchinesische Bronzen*, Berlin, 1924, Pl. 154.

34 LAMP IN FORM OF A RAM
*Han Dynasty, 206 B.C. – A.D. 221*
*Bronze* H. 3 7/8 in. (9.8 cm.); l. 5 in. (12.7 cm.)  931.13.110

Reversible lamp (*lu lu têng*) in form of kneeling ram. The movable
half of the cover is hinged at the back of the neck and can be turned
backwards over the head, forming an oil cup. There is a spike at the
bottom of the interior, to which the wick would have been attached.
The animal is conceived in the round, with individual details on body,
lid and head rendered by incised lines.

CF. M. R. Allen, 'Early Chinese Lamps,' *Oriental Art*, Vol. II, No. 4,
Spring, 1950, p. 139, Fig. 12; M. Fedderson, *Chinese Decorative Art*,
New York, 1961, Fig. 128; *Sekai Bijutsu Zenshū*, Vol. 7, Tokyo, 1952,
Pl. 19; O. Sirén, *A History of Early Chinese Art*, Vol. II, London, 1930,
Pl. 33 A; M. Loehr, *Relics of Ancient China*, Asia House, New York,
1965, Pl. 136.

PUBL.: H. Trubner, *The Arts of the Han Dynasty*, Chinese Art Society
of America, Asia House, New York, 1961, No. 54; *Archives*, Vol. XIV,
1960, p. 37.

35 TOMB TILE

*Former Han Dynasty, 2nd–1st century B.C. From Chin-ts'un*
*Gray pottery with stamped designs  H. 21 in. (53.3 cm.); l. 54 in.*
*(137. 1 cm.)*  931.13.136

Hollow, rectangular tile decorated on both faces with stamped
designs of trees, horses, stag, hound, cranes and flying geese. Four
small does are seen between trees. Border of interlaced T's. Clay
tiles of this type, of which the Museum has a very extensive collection, were commonly used in Han times to line the walls of
underground tomb chambers. They could be produced more cheaply
and more easily than carved stone slabs, as illustrated by the Later
Han reliefs from the tomb of General Tso Yüan-i (No. 37). The
decorative motifs on the stamped tiles, which include hunting
scenes, trees, birds in flight, as well as armed figures carrying
various weapons, provide a rich pictorial representation of the
life and customs of the Han people.

36 TOMB TILE

*Later Han Dynasty, A.D. 25-221*
*Gray pottery  H. 36 in. (91.4 cm.); w. 24 3/4 in. (62.8 cm.)*
931.13.109

Hollow tile in form of section of wall of an edifice with tiled and
gabled roofs. Head, horns and forelegs of a stag modelled in high
relief in the centre, the walls to either side showing pillars and
beams in low relief. Stamped decoration of geometric patterns and
horse-drawn chariots in centre and on back of tile; square with
*t'ao-t'ieh* mask and ring on left and right of the stag's head. Plain,
slightly recessed sides with large hole in centre, presumably for
joining to adjacent tiles lining tomb wall.

PUBL.: H. Trubner, *Arts of the Han Dynasty*, Chinese Art Society
of America, Asia House, New York, 1961, No. 5; *Archives*, Vol.
XIV, 1960, p. 24.

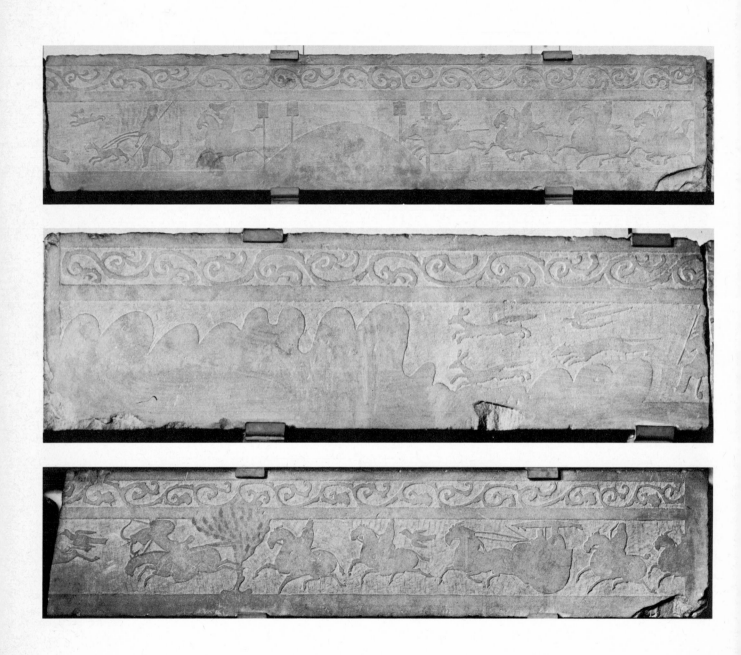

OPPOSITE

37 TOMB RELIEFS
*Later Han Dynasty, dated* A.D. *150   From the tomb of General Tso
Yüan-i, Li-shih district, Shansi.*
*Reddish brown stone   H. (925.25.22 a and b) 14 1/5 in. (36.2 cm.);
l. 121 1/16 in in. (3 m. 7.6 cm.)   H. (925.25.22 l) 14 1/4. (36.2 cm.);
l. 66 15/16 in. (1 m. 70 cm.)*

The three slabs form part of a group consisting of fourteen horizontal stones and two upright pillars. The latter are inscribed and
establish the stones as coming from the tomb of General Tso
Yüan-i, in the Li-shih district, Shansi, reported to have been built
in the first year of the Ho-p'ing era (corresponding to A.D. 150).
The slabs are decorated with hunting scenes, processions of chariots
and horsemen and mythological figures. Two of the details illustrated here, from a long slab broken in two, depict a hunting
scene. They show, from right to left, the curved outline of a
bridge, guarded by a pair of posts at each end, a falconer on
horseback and other riders, a hunter on foot leading a dog, a
second hunter on foot, fleeing animals and a bird, all moving
towards a range of mountains on the far left. The other fragment
shows a procession of horsemen, a tree with massive foliage and a
mounted archer on a horse in 'flying gallop' aiming his arrow at his
fleeing quarry. The tree thus serves as a separation between the
procession and a hunting scene. Thre is evidence that the pictorial
effect of the relief was originally enhanced by the addition of
painted lines, as indicated by ink markings in the bough of the
tree, some of the chariot wheels, reins and other details.

PUBL.: H. Trubner, 'Aspects of Han Pictorial Representation,'
*Transactions of the Oriental Ceramic Society,* Vol. 33, 1960-61,
1961-62, Pls. 27 a-b, and 29 b; T. A. Heinrich, *Art Treasures in the
Royal Ontario Museum,* Toronto, 1963, p. 32 (925.25.22 a).

38 VASE *(hu)*
*Former Han Dynasty, 206* B.C. – A.D. *24*
*Proto-porcelain   H. 15 3/16 in. (38.5 cm.)   920.1.182*

High-fired porcellaneous stoneware with olive-green glaze on lip
and interior of mouth, lower part of neck and shoulder, the lower
body burnt reddish brown. On shoulder, two borders with freely
incised and stippled design of sweeping lines and volutes, separated
by angular ridges; combed pattern at top and base of neck. Hatched
handles with rings attached and two double spirals above.

CF. W. Hochstadter, 'Pottery and Stoneware of Shang, Chou and
Han,' *B.M.F.E.A.,* Vol. 24, 1952, pp. 98-103, and Pl. 29, No. 115;
Daisy Lion Goldschmidt, *Chinese Art,* tr. by Jean-Claude Moreau-
Gobard, New York, 1960. Pl. 169.

**39 VASE**
*Han Dynasty, 206 B.C. – A.D. 221*
*Proto-porcelain H. 15 13/32 in. (39.1 cm.); dia. at mouth
2 15/16 in. (7.5 cm.) 926.21.168*

Vase with narrow, elongated neck, wide flange below mouth.
Ovoid body with two moulded loop handles combined with
t'ao-t'ieh masks in relief on shoulder. The shape of the vase
derives from a bronze prototype. The body, of porcellaneous
stoneware of heavy reddish clay, is covered with feldspathic
glaze of olive-brown tone, sprayed on from above and stopping
short of the shoulder; some streaks of glaze run down over the
lower part of the jar, which is burnt a warm dark brown.

**40 VASE** *(hu)*
*Han Dynasty, 206 B.C. – A.D. 221*
*Pottery with green glaze turning slightly olive on collar H. 14 7/16
in. (36.7 cm.); dia. at mouth 5 5/8 in. (14.4 cm.) 918.21.384*

Red pottery jar with globular body, cylindrical neck and collared
mouth. Jar covered with green glaze turning slightly olive on collar;
a few patches of silvery film where iridescence is beginning. Large
drop of glaze on mouth rim, also three spur marks. On shoulder,
low-relief band with moulded decoration and two t'ao-t'ieh masks in
applied relief with ring handles in style of Han bronze vessels. Relief
band decorated with motifs of running and contending animals, a
mounted hunter turning in his saddle and shooting backwards in
nomadic fashion, men chasing animals, as well as camel-hump mountains and primitive representations of trees. The motif of contending
animals and mounted hunters in full pursuit riding horses in 'flying
gallop' occurs frequently in the repertoire of Han pictorial art and
suggests the influence of the Scythian nomads roaming the steppes
of Central Asia.

CF. S. Okuda, ed., *Chūgoku no Tōji*, Tokyo, 1955, p. 7, Fig. 19.

PUBL.: H. Trubner, *Arts of the Han Dynasty*, Chinese Art Society of
America, Asia House, New York, 1961, No. 21; *Archives*, Vol. XIV,
1960, p. 27.

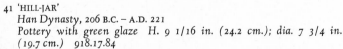

41 'HILL-JAR'
Han Dynasty, 206 B.C. – A.D. 221
*Pottery with green glaze  H. 9 1/16 in. (24.2 cm.); dia. 7 3/4 in. (19.7 cm.)  918.17.84*

Reddish clay with dark green lead silicate glaze; silvery iridescence. Cylindrical body supported on three feet in form of bears. Lid in form of stylized overlapping peaks, symbolizing the Isles of the Blest, the P'eng-lai, of Taoist mythology. Moulded design of contending and galloping animals and phoenix-like birds in flight decorates lid. Around side of body a moulded relief band with design of running and fighting animals, some in contorted poses with their heads turned backward, suggesting violent movement. Monkeys can also be recognized.

CF. R. L. Hobson, *Chinese Pottery and Porcelain*, Vol. I, London, 1915, Pl. 12; B. Laufer, *Pottery of the Han Dynasty*, Leiden, 1909, pp. 174 ff.; A. Wenley, 'The Question of the Po-shan-hsiang-lu,' *Archives*, Vol. III, 1948-49, pp. 5 ff.; M. Sullivan, 'On the Origin of Landscape Representation in Chinese Art,' *Archives*, Vol. VII, 1953, pp. 54 ff.

42 TOMB FIGURE OF A LADY
Later Han Dynasty, A.D. 25-221
*Gray pottery  H. 14 in. (36 cm.); w. at base 6 in. (15.2 cm.)  920.1.199*

Slender figure in frontal pose wearing tight fitting garment which flares out at feet. Hands held together in front and tucked into sleeves of undergarment. Hair parted in centre, falling down back and gathered in knot.

For similar tomb figures. CF. *Ch'üan-kuo chi-pên chien shê kung-ch'êng chung ch'u-t'u wên-wu chan-lan t'u-lu*, (Construction Sites), Vol. I, Pl. 63; *K'ao-ku*, 1959, No. 12, Pl. 5, Figs. 1-3 (from Shansi); *Shan-tung wen-wu hsuan-chi* (Selection of Cultural Relics in Shantung), pp. 86-87, Figs. 167-168.

PUBL.: H. Trubner, *Arts of the Han Dynasty*, Chinese Art Society of America, Asia House, New York, 1961, No. 30; *Archives*, Vol. XIV, 1960, p. 31.

**43 GROUP OF BURIAL FIGURES**
*Said to have come from Ma-p'o, Mang-shan, near Lo-yang, Honan*
*Northern Wei Dynstay, dated* A.D. *525*
*Gray pottery with coloured pigments over white undercoating*
*920.5.35 ff. 922.9*

The Museum has more than a hundred of these figures, which are
said to have come from the burial, in A.D. 525, of two brothers, both
princes of the royal house. The inscribed memorial slab reportedly
found with the figures stated that the brothers were executed in
519 after having been accused of rebellion. When they were later

pardoned, the bodies are said to have been removed to Lo-yang and
given an honourable burial. The two groups of figures may have
been intended to represent the state funeral then accorded to the
two brothers.
The inscribed tomb slab was unfortunately not included in the ship-
ment of the figures to the Royal Ontario Museum in 1920.

Documentation found with the figures has been published by Chao
Wan-li, 'Han Wei Nan Pei ch'ao mu chih shih', K'ao ku hsüeh
chuan k'an, Series B. No. 2, Peking, 1956, Vol. I, pp. 28-29 and Vol.
III, Pls. 34 and 40.

**44** THREE BURIAL FIGURES
*Said to have come from the extreme western part of Honan*
*6th – 7th century*
*Gray pottery with traces of paint over white undercoating*
*Standing figure (920.1.25) h. 16 1/2 in. (41.9 cm.) Standing*
*figure (920.1.26) h. 16 1/2 in. (41.9 cm.) Seated figure (920.1.31)*
*h. 16 3/8 in. (41.6 cm.)*

The relaxed poses of these figures and the delicate, rather soft treatment of their faces suggest a possible influence from the art of the
Central Asian Buddhist kingdoms then lying between India and
China. They are part of an unusual group of tomb figures in the
Museum's collection, distinguished by the use of supporting iron
armatures inside the clay bodies, apparently a technical innovation of this period. Superficial similarities of features and types
between these figures and some of the stucco sculptures from
Tumshuq, Central Asia, should be noted.

CF. L. Hambis, *Toumchouq*, Mission Paul Pelliot, Vol. I, *Planches*,
Paris, 1961, Pl. LXXV, Fig. 183 (right figure); Pl. LXXVI, Fig. 185 (note
formation and treatment of beard); Pl. CXLV, Fig. 425 (Shōrchuk:
treatment of eyes and brows).

PUBL.: P. Ghent, 'Secrets of Ancient Chinese Pottery Revealed by
X-Ray,' *Canadian X-ray Newsletter*, Vol. 5, No. 1 (n.d.); H. É.
Fernald, 'Discovery of Iron Armatures and Supports in Chinese
Grave Figurines of the 6th and early 7th Centuries,' *Far Eastern
Ceramic Bulletin*, No. 11, Sept., 1950, pp. 105-108; W. Todd, 'Iron
Armatures and Supports in Chinese Grave Figurines,' *R.O.M.A.
Bulletin*, No. 18, March, 1952, pp. 17-18; T. A. Heinrich, *Art
Treasures in The Royal Ontario Museum*, Toronto, 1963, p. 37
(920.1.25).

42

**45** BUDDHIST STELE
*Northern Wei Dynasty, dated* A.D.523  *From southern Shansi or Shensi*

*Reddish sandstone  H. 88 1/2 in. (224.8 cm.); w. 27 in. (68.55 cm.)*
949.100

Central pavilion occupied by a seated Buddha, the right hand in
*abhaya mudrā* ('fear not'), the left in *varada mudrā* ('compassion'),
and two Bodhisattvas standing on lotus pedestals. The relief above
depicts the Great Departure of Prince Siddhartha from the royal
palace, riding on a horse whose hooves are supported by two apsarases. The city of Kapilavastu is represented in map-like fashion,
enclosing the scene of the Departure. At the base are two seated
donors in niches, each confronted by a servant, and, below, five
standing donors.
The reverse side shows a Buddhist trinity, partly destroyed, at the
top, above a pavilion with seated figure and servant, flanked by
three standard bearers on the outside. A similar arrangement, but
with two pavilions, is shown below, followed in turn by rows of
donors.

PUBL.: O. Sirén, 'La Sculpture Chinoise à l'exposition de l'Orangerie,'
*Revue des Arts Asiatiques*, Vol. XI, No. 1, 1937, Pl. 1; G. Salles 'Arts
de la Chine Ancienne,' Exhibition Catalogue, Paris, 1937, Pl. VI,
No. 10; H. E. Fernald, 'Some Chinese Sculpture at the Orangerie,'
*Burlington Magazine*, Vol. LXXI, Oct., 1937, pp. 184-187; *An Exhibi-
tion of Chinese Stone Sculptures*, C. T. Loo & Co., New York, 1940,
Pl. XIII, No. 17; R. Grousset, *La Chine et son Art*, Paris, 1951, p. 101;
H. E. Fernald, 'A Chinese Buddhist Sculpture,' *R.O.M.A. Bulletin*,
No. 18, March, 1952, pp. 4-8, Figs. 1, 2 and 3; T. A. Heinrich, *Art
Treasures in the Royal Ontario Museum*, Toronto, 1963, p. 39.

46 DEMON
*Northern Ch'i Dynasty, A.D. 550-577    From the Buddhist cave-temples
at Hsiang-t'ang Shan, Honan
Dark gray limestone   H. 31 in. (78.7. cm.)   960.92*

Figure of squatting demon in high relief. It is carved from the solid
stone of one of the rock-cut cave-temples at Hsiang-t'ang Shan and
originally served as a caryatid or architectural support at the entrance
or inside a sanctuary.

CF.  S. Mizuno and T. Nagahiro, *The Buddhist Cave-Temples of
Hsiang-t'ang-ssu*, Kyoto, 1937, Pls. LVII A, LVIII C-D.

PUBL.: H. Trubner, 'A Demon from Hsiang-t'ang Shan,' *Annual*, Art
and Archaeology Division, ROM, 1961, pp. 73-74; T. A. Heinrich, *Art
Treasures in the Royal Ontario Museum*, Toronto, 1963, p. 37.

44

47 AMITĀBHA BUDDHA
*Northern Ch'i Dynasty, dated* A.D.577  *From west-central Hopei*
*White marble*  H. 105 3/4 in. (268.6 cm.)  923.18.13

The figure is carved in the micaceous white marble characteristic of
the region of Ting-chou and Pao-ting in west-central Hopei, southwest of Peking. The right hand, now missing, was originally raised
in *abhaya mudrā* ('fear not'). The base, consisting of a low drum
decorated with lotus leaves in high relief, is typical of sculptures of
this school. The drum, in turn, rests upon a rectangular plinth,
which is inscribed and contains the date corresponding to A.D. 577.
The sculpture reflects considerable influence of Indian art of the
Gupta period, notably in the close-fitting robe which suggests the
modelling of the body underneath, and in the parallel, thin ridges
of folds, reminiscent of the parallel folds of Indian sculpture of the
school of Mathurā.

PUBL.: L. Sickman and A. Soper, *The Art and Architecture of China*,
Harmondsworth, 1956, Pl. 45 A; T. A. Heinrich, *Art Treasures in the
Royal Ontario Museum*, Toronto, 1963, p. 41.

48  BODHISATTVA
*T'ang Dynasty, late 7th–8th century. From the Buddhist cave-temples at T'ien-lung Shan, Shansi*
*Gray sandstone  H. 29 1/2 in. (69.85 cm.)  Purchased with funds from the Reuben Wells Leonard Bequest, 953.127.*

This figure of a Bodhisattva originally formed part of a large Buddhist group in one of the cave-temples at T'ien-lung Shan. It is characterized by strong Indian influence, reflected in the swaying pose and semi-nude form. Flowing scarves fall over the shoulders and another scarf, draped over the left arm, falls across the front of the figure. The body, naked to the waist, and the head and neck are distinguished by full modelling and a deliberate contrast between the soft flesh and hardness of the jewelry, a feature also found in Indian sculpture. The treatment of the thin, close-fitting skirt or *dhoti* is also very Indian in that it reveals the modelling of the body underneath.

PUBL.: *Exhibition of Ancient Chinese Bronzes and Buddhist Art,* Yamanaka and Co., New York, 1938, No. 58; 'West-East,' *R.O.M.A. Bulletin,* No. 21, Oct., 1953, No. 109; T. A. Heinrich, *Art Treasure in the Royal Ontario Museum,* Toronto, 1963, p. 41.

49  SIDE OF MORTUARY BED
*Six Dynasties period, second half of 6th century*

*Dark gray limestone  H. 19 3/8 in. (49.2 cm.); l. 82 3/4 in. (210.2 cm.)  Purchased in part with funds from the Reuben Wells Leonard Bequest, 949.230.*

Decorated in low relief with five fantastic creatures biting a double band. Monster in centre, flanked by two dragon-like animals and pair of fantastic birds. Central support with two human figures leaning on staffs. Monster-like animals depicted on two side supports.

PUBL.: *An Exhibition of Chinese Stone Sculptures,* C. T. Loo & Co., New York 1940, Pl. XXVII, No. 35; T. A. Heinrich, *Art Treasures in the Royal Ontario Museum,* Toronto, 1963, p. 38.

50 EWER
*T'ang Dynasty, 618-906   Reportedly from Lo-yang, Honan*
*Pottery with mottled green, yellow and transparent glazes   H. 9 1/2*
*in. (24.15 cm.)   920.1.83*

The shape, with narrow contracted mouth and double-strand handle, derives from a Near Eastern metal prototype. The decoration in applied relief, which includes a semi-nude dancer and dragon-like animal, shows strong 'Irano-Hellenistic' influence. Both form and decoration illustrate the frequent intrusion of Iranian and Western Asiatic motifs upon the art of T'ang China.

PUBL.: O. Sirén, *Kinas Konst under tre Årtusenden*, Vol. II, Stockholm, 1943, p. 200, Fig. 229; 'West-East,' *R.O.M.A. Bulletin*, No. 21, Oct., 1953, No. 115; T. Drexel, *Die Formen Chinesischer Keramik*, Tübingen, 1955, Pl. 49 b; *The Arts of the T'ang Dynasty*, Los Angeles County Museum, 1957, No. 186.

51 BUDDHIST ALTARPIECE
*T'ang Dynasty, 7th – 8th century*
*Gilt bronze   H. 12 1/8 in. (30.8 cm.)   958.81*

The stand and figures apparently do not belong together, for the inscription on the stand gives a date corresponding to A.D. 582, whereas the Buddha and elaborate openwork mandorla with flying apsarases clearly reflect the mature T'ang style of the late seventh and first half of the eighth century. The small altarpiece is, however, an excellent example of this type of ritual object, made in large numbers for individual household shrines during the T'ang Dynasty.

T'ang Dynasty, 618-906
*Pottery with green, amber and straw-coloured yellow glazes*
*H. 28 1/4 in. (71.7 cm.)   918.21.290*

Horse with pale, straw-coloured yellow glaze, relieved by brilliant
green of saddle cloth and palmette-shaped medallions, and by amber
glaze of harness and straps. It is an excellent example of the high
degree of technical perfection and sculptural qualities achieved in
the best of the tomb figures of the seventh and eighth centuries.

48

**53 JAR**
*T'ang Dynasty, 618-906*
*Pottery with 'three-colour' glazes   H. 7 9/16 in. (19.2 cm.)   928.31.1*

This jar is distinguished by its bold shape with ovoid, swelling body and wide shoulders contracted at the neck. A cream-coloured glaze covers the body and terminates in an uneven line below the waist, a characteristic feature of T'ang ceramics. Foliate medallions with green, amber and cream glazes, and separated from each other by a chevron pattern in green. Amber glaze also covers the mouth and neck.

PUBL.: T. A. Heinrich, *Art Treasures in the Royal Ontario Museum*, Toronto, 1963, pp. 52-53.

**54 MERCHANT HOLDING WINE SKIN VESSEL**
*T'ang Dynasty, 618-906*
*Pottery with 'three-colour' amber, green and cream glazes, partially mottled and streaked   H. 14 3/8 in. (63.5 cm.)   918.21.7*

Two other figures of similar type are known, one in the Museum of Fine Arts, Boston, the other in the Seattle Art Museum (J. G. Mahler, *The Westerners among the Figurines of the T'ang Dynasty of China*, Rome, 1959, Pls. III a-d). The Toronto figure and the two related examples all represent foreigners with strong Armenoid traits, distinguished by beak-like noses, deep-set eyes peering out from under heavy brows, and thick, heavy hair. They wear tunics of Persian type and each carries a wine skin vessel.

PUBL.: 'West-East,' *R.O.M.A. Bulletin*, No. 21, 1953, No. 3; Mahler, *op. cit.*, Pl. III e.

55 RHYTON CUP
*T'ang Dynasty, 618-906*
*Pottery with 'three-colour' amber, green and cream glazes   H. 2 15/16*
*in. (7.45 cm.); l. 4 1/2 in. (11.45 cm.)   920.20.1*

Rhyton cup in form of Chinese citron flower with nomadic figure riding on top.

PUBL.: 'West-East,' *R.O.M.A. Bulletin*, No. 21, Oct., 1953, No. 120; *The Arts of the T'ang Dynasty*, Los Angeles County Museum, 1957, No. 215.

56 STEM CUP
*T'ang Dynasty, 618-906*
*Porcelain with thin, bluish-white glaze, almost of ch'ing-p'ai type*
*H. 3 5/16 in. (8.4 cm.); dia. of mouth 3 5/16 in. (8.4 cm.); dia. of*
*base 1 9/16 in. (4 cm.)   921.21.2*

True procelain – white, translucent and emitting a sound when struck – was made in China as early as the T'ang Dynasty. Fragments of T'ang porcelain have been found in the ruins of Samarra, the ancient city on the Tigris, in Mesopotamia, founded in 836 and abandoned in 883. The stem cup provides important proof of the production of porcelain in China, roughly a thousand years before the secrets of porcelain making were discovered in the West. The piece is similar to a stem cup in the collection of Sir Alan and Lady Barlow, in England.

CF. *The Arts of the T'ang Dynasty*, Oriental Ceramic Society, London, 1955, No. 189; *The Arts of the T'ang Dynasty*, Los Angeles County Museum, 1957, No. 236; M. Sullivan, *Chinese Ceramics, Bronzes and Jades in the Collection of Sir Alan and Lady Barlow*, London, 1963, No. 26 c.

PUBL.: T. A. Heinrich, *Art Treasures in the Royal Ontario Museum*, Toronto, 1963, p. 58.

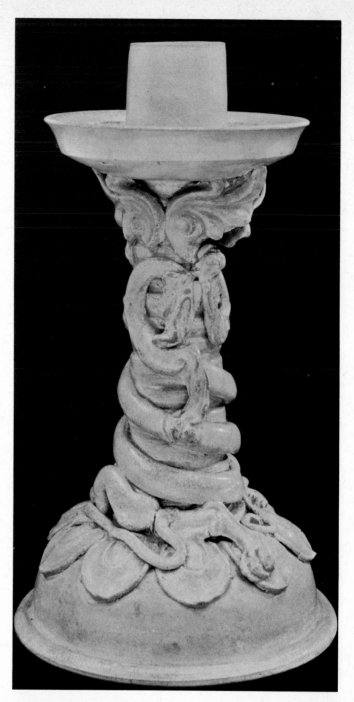

57 VASE
*T'ang Dynasty, 618-906*
*Porcelain with cream-coloured glaze   H. 13 in. (33.1 cm.)   923.18.14*

Ovoid body with narrow, ribbed neck and flaring mouth with up-
turned lip. Deep groove with loop-guide at top and bottom,
apparently to hold side straps, on either side of vessel.

PUBL.: T. Drexel, *Die Formen Chinesischer Keramik*, Tübingen, 1955,
Pl. 38 a; *The Arts of the T'ang Dynasty*, Los Angeles County Museum,
1957, No. 218; T. A. Heinrich, *Art Treasures in the Royal Ontario
Museum*, Toronto, 1963, p. 58.

58 CANDLESTICK
*T'ang Dynasty, 618-906*

*Pottery with transparent neutral glaze   H. 11 7/8 in. (29.9 cm.)*
*903.65.3*

Cylindrical stem rising from bell-shaped base, decorated with petals
in relief. Two dragons coiled around stem and paired acanthus
leaves supporting saucer at top. The influence of Near Eastern art
is evident in the acanthus leaves and the petal motif.

PUBL.: T. Kobayashi, *Tōsō no hakuji*, Tōki Zenshū, Vol. 12, Tokyo,
1959, Pl. 3; T. A. Heinrich, *Art Treasures in the Royal Ontario
Museum*, Toronto, 1963, p. 58.

59 AMPHORA
*T'ang Dynasty, 618-906*
*Stoneware with transparent neutral glaze H. 19 3/4 in. (50.15 cm.)*
918.21.192

Hellenistic shape, with two handles in form of dragons biting the rim. Glaze applied over white slip and terminating in wavy line short of base.

60 SEATED LION
*T'ang Dynasty, 618-906*
*Pottery with thin, transparent glaze H. 9 1/2 in. (24.1 cm.)*
918.21.397

Slip-covered pottery with neutral glaze, partially covered with silvery iridescence. The lion is closely related to similar examples in stone and marble. One of the finest examples in white marble is in the Nelson Gallery, Kansas City (Sickman and Soper, *op. cit.*, Pl. 61 B), but the ceramic lion in Toronto displays equally strong sculptural qualities, suggestive of more monumental works in stone. There is also a small, white marble lion in the Royal Ontario Museum (Acc. No. 933.12.4) which forms an interesting comparison to the pottery example.

PUBL.: T. Kobayashi, *Tōsō no hakuji*, Tōki Zenshū, Vol. 12, Tokyo, 1959, Pl. 4.

**62 BOWL AND COVER**
*T'ang Dynasty, 618-906*
*Beaten silver, chased and gilt decoration   Ht. 3 7/8 in. (9.8 cm.); dia.
9 3/4 in. (24.7 cm.)   960.9.129*

**61 STEM CUP**
*T'ang Dynasty, 618-906*
*Gilt bronze   H. 2 9/16 in. (6.5 cm.); dia. of stand 1 1/8 in. (2.9
cm.); dia. of mouth 2 1/4 in. (5.4 cm.)   950.36.3*

Gilt bronze stem cup of egg-cup shape, with slightly everted foot.
The shape originated in Persia but is frequently found in China in
the T'ang and later periods. The exterior is decorated at the top
with a floral and cloud band below the lip. A wide band around the
body shows hunting scenes with riders on galloping horses, inter-
spersed with leaping deer in a landscape. The motif of the 'flying
gallop' was originally derived from Scythian art of about the
second century B.C. and from the art of the Ordos region, for the
nomads of this area excelled in hunting. The lower body is decorated with a zig-zag border above a triple petal design. The stem
shows floral or cloud motifs, while the concave base has plant and
mountain designs. The decoration is generally chased or engraved on
a ground of regular ring matting against a background of rows of
tiny, punched circles, a technique borrowed from Sassanian metalwork.

C.F. O. Sirén, *A History of Early Chinese Art*, Vol. II, London, 1930,
pp. 23-32; B. Gyllensvard, *Chinese Gold and Silver in the Carl Kempe
Collection*, Stockholm, 1953, No. 109; *The Arts of the T'ang Dynasty*,
Los Angeles County Museum, 1957, No. 342 (silver); 'T'ang Gold and
Silver,' B.M.F.E.A., Vol. 29, 1957, Pl. 17 a; T. Misugi ed., *Old Chinese
Art*. Osaka, 1961, text facing No. 14, and illustrations, No. 27.

PUBL.: M. Sullivan, *Introduction to Chinese Art*, London, 1961, p. 130.

Six-lobed bowl and cover, with everted rims soldered to foot and
cover. The cover, if reversed, may be used as a saucer and has an
overlapping edge. The form is closely related to multi-lobed bowls of
Persian prototype, but is distinctively T'ang and its shape inspired by
the Buddhist lotus. Both bowl and cover are decorated with floral
sprays, each consisting of a circle of four separate sprays of lotus
flowers and pomegranates. The border decoration, with overlapping
petals, is of Sassanian derivation, and of a type frequently used during
the later T'ang period.
A similar bowl and cover, in the Carl Kempe Collection in Sweden,
comes from a tomb near Pa-lin in Eastern Mongolia, a site where eight
similar bowls, four with cover and four without, were discovered.
Similar bowls are found in the following collections: the M. Mansson
Collection, Stockholm; Hultmard Collection, Stockholm; Hellström
Collection, Sweden (bowl only); University Museum, Philadelphia
(two sets); Seattle Art Museum (two sets).

CF. B. Gyllensvard, *Chinese Gold and Silver in the Carl Kempe Collection*, Stockholm, 1953, No. 115, pp. 175-176; 'T'ang Silver and Gold,'
B.M.F.E.A. Vol. 29, 1957, Fig. 42 b and Pl. 21.

PUBL.: T. A. Heinrich, *Art Treasures in the Royal Ontario Museum*,
Toronto, 1963, pp. 48-49.

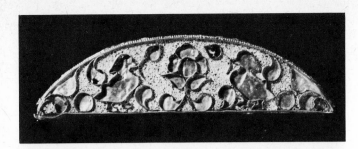

63 COMB TOP

*T'ang Dynasty, 618-906*
*Gold filigree H. 3/4 in. (1.9 cm.); l. 2 31/32 in. (7.5 cm.) Gift of Mrs. Edgar J. Stone, 959.120.1*

Comb top made of two sheets of gold with birds and floral design in raised cloisons on finely granulated ground; originally inlaid with turquoise. Design of standing birds on one side, birds in flight on the other. The motif of birds picking flowers was a popular theme, frequently employed during the T'ang dynasty, and can be seen on some of the treasures in the Shōsōin, Japan. The motif was apparently introduced from Persia, for corresponding designs can be found in Sassanian art.

CF. *Nihon Bijutsu Jiten* (Dictionary of Japanese Art), Tokyo, 1952, p. 509; B. Gyllensvard, *Chinese Gold and Silver in the Carl Kempe Collection*, Stockholm, 1953, No. 37; 'T'ang Gold and Silver,' B.M.F.E.A., Vol. 29, 1957, Figs. 64, 69, p. 116.

64 HAIR PIN

*Late T'ang or early Sung Dynasty*
*Beaten silver L. 12 7/8 in. (32.7 cm.); w. (greatest) 2 3/16 in. (5.5 cm.) Gift of Mrs. Edgar J. Stone, 959.117.2*

Hair pin of beaten silver of the type *tsun*, with rounded ornamental end. Wider part embellished with rich openwork and chased design of phoenix among lotus scrolls extending from mouth of dragon. Narrow part merges into flat, bifurcated pin. Both the dragon and phoenix were auspicious symbols. Metalwork, which was introduced to China in the Warring States period, came to flourish in T'ang China. The elaborate openwork design of this piece reflects the luxurious and decorative nature of T'ang work, greatly favoured by the court. Gilt openwork was popular in T'ang China, as indicated by examples in the Shōsōin, at Nara, Japan, where the portion of a crown and other objects, very similar in style and theme to the present piece, are preserved.

CF. *Exhibition of Chinese Art*, C.T. Loo and Co., New York, 1942, No. 216; B. Gyllensvard, *Chinese Gold and Silver in the Carl Kempe Collection*, Stockholm, 1953, No. 126; 'T'ang Gold and Silver,' B.M.F.E.A., Vol. 29, 1957, p. 37; *The Arts of the T'ang Dynasty*, Los Angeles County Museum, 1957, No. 358.

PUBL.: T.A. Heinrich, *Art Treasures in the Royal Ontario Museum*, Toronto, 1963, pp. 48-49.

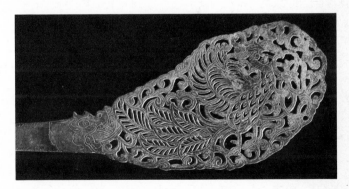

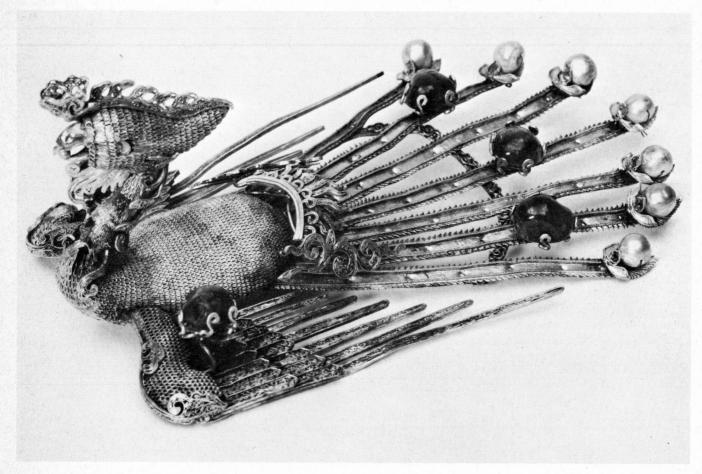

65  HAIR ORNAMENT
*Sung Dynasty, 960-1279*
*Gold filigree with pearls and cabochon rubies  Lee of Fareham Collection, permanent loan from the Massey Foundation, L.960.9.124.*

Male phoenix *(fêng)* in minutely executed gold filigree work. It is shown in flight with extended wings and tail feathers, and raised head. The head and body of the bird are made of thin plaited gold wires which are soldered together. The beak is solid gold, while the crest and the decoration at the base of the tail are in filigree work in cloud and flame-like motifs. The body is built on a framework of strong wires. There are small openings for the eyes. The wings are in filigree at the base, and are extended by seven thin bands on each of which the twisted wire is attached along the contours. A cabochon ruby decorates each wing at its centre. There are seven tail feathers which are soldered to a small fan. At the end of each feather is a pearl in a leaf-shaped receptacle, while in the centre of every second feather a cabochon ruby is attached. Originally the bird probably formed part of a crown.

The phoenix symbol, male and female *(fêng* and *huang)*, which was used during and after the T'ang dynasty, is the special symbol of the empress and was commonly employed to embellish the hair.
Similar birds are in the possession of the following collections: Metropolitan Museum of Art, New York; Mr. Zensuke Fuji, Kyoto, Japan; Dr. Carl Kempe, Stockholm.

CF. *Chinese Art in the Collection of Mr. Zensuke Fuji, Kyoto*, n.p., n.d., No. 42; *Ausstellung Chinesischer Kunst*, Berlin, 1929, No. 449; *International Exhibition of Chinese Art*, Illustrated Supplement, London, 1935-36, No. 708; C.T. Loo, *Ancient Chinese Bronzes and Chinese Jewelry*, Toledo Museum of Art, 1941, No. 126; *Exhibition of Chinese Arts*, C.T. Loo & Co., Special Sale, New York, 1941-42, No. 211; B. Gyllensvard, *Chinese Gold and Silver in the Carl Kempe Collection*, Stockholm, 1953, No. 54.

PUBL.: T. A. Heinrich, *Art Treasures in the Royal Ontario Museum*, Toronto, 1963, pp. 48-49.

66 VASE *(mei p'ing)*
*Sung Dynasty, 12th-13th century*
*Tz'u-chou ware   H. 13 7/16 in. (34.1 cm.); dia. 11 7/8 in. (30.2 cm.)*
*918.21.395*

Ovoid body. Two bands of carved floral design above row of overlapping petals cut through deep brown glaze, background filled with buff-white slip.

The Tz'u-chou wares, named after their principal place of manufacture, Tz'u-chou or 'Porcelain Prefecture,' in southern Hopei, represent one of the largest and most important groups of Sung ceramics. Tz'u-chou is a slip-covered stoneware, the use of a slip being a distinguishing feature of the ware. Various decorative designs were applied by painting on the slip, carving or incising through it to expose the clay body underneath, or by a combination of several techniques. A transparent overglaze was subsequently applied over the design. White, black and brown slips and glazes were freely contrasted with each other, sometimes supplemented by the use of coloured over-glaze enamels (No. 13) to produce simple, though strikingly beautiful designs.

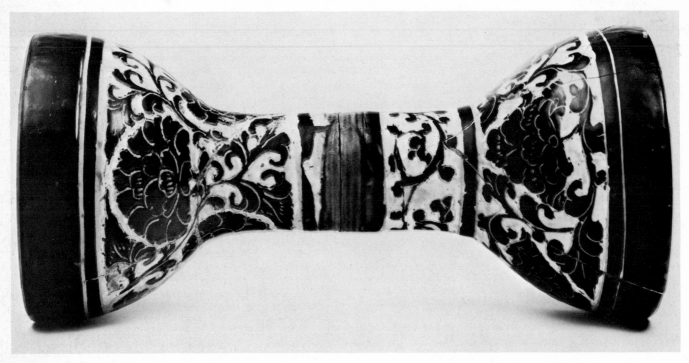

67 BODY OF DRUM
*Sung Dynasty, 960-1279*
*Tz'u-chou ware  L. 14 11/16 in. (37.24 cm.); dia. (greatest) 6 11/16
in. (16.9 cm.)  920.1.209*

Peony design in black and white slip, the black cut away and incised
under transparent glaze.

CF. *Sekai Tōji Zenshū*, Vol. 10, Tokyo, 1955, Pl. 116.

68 FIGURE OF YEN-LO WANG (YAMA),
PRESIDENT OF THE FIFTH COURT OF HADES
*Ming Dynasty, 16th century*
*Porcelain with coloured glazes*  H. 33 in. (83.8 cm.); w. (of base) 28
in. (71.1 cm.)  923.6.3

PUBL.: *The Arts of the Ming Dynasty*, Detroit Institute of Arts, 1952,
No. 212; T. A. Heinrich, *Art Treasures in the Royal Ontario Museum*,
Toronto, 1963, pp. 62-63.

TA-SHIH-CHIH  See caption 75 on page 61.

69 VASE *(mei p'ing)*
*Sung Dynasty, 960-1279*
*Tz'u-chou type*   H. 7 11/16 in. *(19.5 cm.)*   918.21.396

Globular body. Painted decoration of leaf scrolls in iron oxide on tea-dust green glaze.

70 EWER *(handle and spout missing)*
*Sung Dynasty, 11th-12th century*
*Northern Celadon*   H. 11 5/8 in. *(29.5 cm.)*   922.20.79

All-over floral scrolls carved on body and shoulder, row of petals round neck. Two loop handles, each with palmette and combed design on shoulder. Olive-green glaze. Handle and spout both missing, opening for the spout now covered by monster mask in relief.
Northern Celadon comprises a large group of green-glazed wares, widely distributed over Honan and other parts of northern China. The ware is distinguished by a gray porcellaneous body covered with a transparent olive-green to olive-brown glaze, as distinct from the Southern Chekiang or Lung-ch'üan celadons, which usually have a thick, glossy, grayish or bluish-green glaze.

PUBL.: *Tōsetsu*, No. 72, 1959, Pl. 6; T. A. Heinrich, *Art Treasures in the Royal Ontario Museum*, Toronto, 1963, pp. 56-57.

**71 JAR AND COVER**
*Sung Dynasty, 960-1279*
*Ting ware H. 2 7/8 in. (7.3 cm.); dia. (of mouth) 3 7/16 in. (8.35 cm.) 921.21.130*

Buff white porcellaneous ware with rust-brown glaze. CF. *Sekai Tōji Zenshū*, Vol. 10, Tokyo, 1955, No. 70 ('Honan Temmoku').
Ting yao (yao – ware), which was originally made in Hopei, reached its greatest fame early in the twelfth century, but soon lost its imperial patronage to Ju yao. With the fall of the Northern Sung capital in 1127, many of the Ting potters are said to have fled south, where they maintained the manufacture of the ware near Chi-chou, in Kiangsi. The most common Ting yao is a fine, white porcelain, decorated with delicately incised designs, sometimes carved or moulded, under a warm ivory white glaze. However, rarer examples with black or rust-brown glazes, as illustrated by the present example, also occur.

PUBL.: T. A. Heinrich, *Art Treasures in the Royal Ontario Museum*, Toronto, 1963, p. 59.

**72 CUP-STAND**
*Sung Dynasty, 960-1279*
*Ting ware H. 2 1/4 in. (5.2 cm.) 939.28.2*

Small bowl attached to saucer with six-lobed rim and high, spreading foot. Buff-white porcellaneous ware with rust-brown glaze.

CF. 'The Arts of the Sung Dynasty,' *T.O.C.S.* Vol. 32, 1959-60, No. 37.

60

**73 TEA-BOWL**
*Sung Dynasty, 960-1279*
*Chien ware  H. 2 1/2 in. (6.4 cm.); dia. 5 in. (12.7 cm.)  963.141.13*

Conical shape with characteristic small foot. Grayish-black stoneware covered with lustrous black glaze with 'hare's fur' markings. The kiln-site of Chien ware was discovered in Fukien, China's chief tea-growing region, by the late J. M. Plumer. The ware was made for tea-drinking, and consists mostly of tea bowls, similar to the one here illustrated.

**74 JAR OF LOTUS BUD SHAPE**
*Sung Dynasty, 960-1279*
*Chün ware  H. 3 5/16 in. (8.35 cm.)  931.18.11*

Small jar, covered with lavender-gray glaze with bright purple splashes. Small foot, partially glazed.
Chün yao was made in Honan. It is most frequently distinguished by an opalescent glaze of lavender-gray to blue colour, often suffused with large purple splashes. A much rarer type of Chün is covered with a green glaze. This variety usually occurs in the form of small bowls and shallow dishes. The museum has two examples of green Chün.

75 KUAN-YIN (Avalokiteśvara) and TA-SHIH-CHIH (Mahasthamaprapta)
*Chin Dynasty, dated A.D. 1195 From a temple near Hung-tung Hsien,
not far from Kuang-shêng-ssu, South Shansi (see frontispiece)
Polychromed wood   H. 75 5/16 in. (191.3 cm.)   922.4.6 and 7*

The Bodhisattvas, Kuan-yin and Ta-shih-chih, were the favourite
attendants of Amitābha, Buddha of the Western Paradise, and were
frequently shown flanking this deity. Kuan-yin, opposite, personifies
divine compassion and mercy for suffering mankind, and thus became
exceedingly popular throughout the Far East, especially in China and
Japan. Ta-shih-chih (page 57) is the Bodhisattva of wisdom.
The Bodhisattvas are represented in relaxed, slightly swaying poses,
standing on a circular base. They wear voluminous skirts, flowing
scarves and elaborate jewelry over the chest and on the arms. The
hair is dressed in a high top-knot, hidden behind an ornate crown,
the front of which is carved in relief with a small figure supported on
a lotus. The bodies are heavy and fleshy, qualities characteristic of
Sung sculpture, and are distinguished by full, ample modelling.
The inside of both figures was hollowed out from the back and a
wooden tablet was inserted to close the opening. The tablet from the
figure of Kuan-yin, which has been removed, has a twenty-three
character inscription stating that the image was carved in the sixth
year of Ming-ch'ang (A.D. 1195) and was set up in a temple at Hung-
tung Hsien, in the prefecture of P'ing-yang, Shansi. Together with
the companion piece of Ta-shih-chih, which may be assumed to date
from the same year, it once formed a trinity around a central image
of Amitābha.

PUBL.: O. Sirén, *A History of Early Chinese Art*, Vol. III, London,
1929-30, Pls. 110, 113 B; L. Bachhofer, 'Two Chinese Wooden Statues,'
*Burlington Magazine*, Vol. 73, No. 427, Oct., 1938, pp. 142-145; W. C.
White, *Chinese Temple Frescoes, A Study of Three Wall-paintings of
the Thirteenth Century*, Toronto, 1940, Figs. 9 A, B.; L. Bachhofer, *A
Short History of Chinese Art*, New York, 1946, Pl. 76 B; S. Matsubara,
'On the Genealogy of Chinese Sculpture in the Sung and Yüan
Periods,' *Kokka*, No. 833, Aug., 1961, pp. 341-355.

OPPOSITE

76 LOHAN
*Liao—Chin Dynasties, 10th-12th century*
*Pottery with green, yellow and amber glazes* H. 49 3/4 in. (126.3 cm.) 914.4.1

The image represents a Lohan (Sanskrit: *Arhat*; Japanese: *Rakan*), a disciple of the Buddha. It formed part of a larger group of similar figures, now scattered among different collections in America, Japan and England, originally set up in a cave temple near I-chou, in Hopei Province. It is made of high-fired clay, covered with green, yellow and amber glazes. The head, which was broken off and later repaired, has acquired a brownish stain, which is deepest on the upper portion and was perhaps caused by water dripping from the roof of the cave. The figure portrays an Indian monk. The eyes are coloured black and the hair is shaved. The drapery consists of a green robe, tied around the waist with a thin, yellow sash, and an outer robe of the same colour. Over the outer robe there is a garment worn especially by monks (Japanese: *kesa*), coloured orange-yellow and partitioned by broad bands, which are edged with green and ornamented with white quatrefoil or plum blossom designs on a yellow ground. This drapery covers both shoulders and legs, and is tied behind the neck.
The seat, with its sides cut out in open-work, suggests a rocky ledge. The top of the seat is glazed green, but at the sides, the green is lightly mottled with white and yellow.
The Arhats, known as Lohans in China, are Buddhist disciples. Their number, originally sixteen, was subsequently increased to eighteen and, in Japan, to five hundred or more. Under the two Tartar dynasties of Liao and Chin, from the tenth to the thirteenth century, a very active school of Buddhism flourished in north China, resulting in the manufacture of numerous polychromed sculptures of wood and clay. The naturalistic tendencies of this period were much stronger than in earlier times, as reflected in the life-like qualities of the present figure. Other figures of the same series are in the British Museum, Museum of Fine Arts, Boston, Metropolitan Museum of Art, New York, University Museum, Philadelphia, William Rockhill Nelson Gallery, Kansas City and the Matsukata collection in Japan.

CF. A. Priest, *Chinese Sculpture in the Metropolitan Museum of Art*, New York, 1944, pls. CXXIV, CXXV, Cat. Nos. 73-74; L. Sickman and A. Soper, *The Art and Architecture of China*, Harmondsworth, 1956, pp. 101-102, Pls. 81 B, 83 B; *Handbook, Nelson Gallery of Art – Atkins Museum*, Kansas City, 1959, p. 191.

PUBL.: T. A. Heinrich, *Art Treasures in the Royal Ontario Museum*, Toronto, 1963, p. 55.

77 EWER
*Liao Dynasty, 916-1124*
*Pottery with green glaze* H. 4 3/4 in. (18.5 cm.) 959.84

Moulded and incised decoration of shells. Flat, square plaque with monster mask moulded in relief applied to one side. This ewer and the two items, 79 and 80, illustrate the ceramic art of the Liao Dynasty, established by the Khitan or Tartar rulers of Manchuria. The bodies and glazes of the Liao wares generally show close affinities with the T'ang wares.

78 PILLOW
*Liao Dynasty, 916-1124*
*Pottery with green and yellow glazes over white slip; carved floral*
*design in central medallion.  H. 5 3/8 in. (13.7 cm.); l. 15 3/4 in.*
*(40 cm.); w. 10 15/16 in. (27.75 cm.)   918.21.501*

79 VASE WITH PHOENIX HEAD
*Liao Dynasty, 916-1124*
*Pottery with white and green glazes  H. 16 7/8 in. (42.8 cm.)*
*918.21.472*

The shape is characteristic of ceramics of the Liao Dynasty and is
distinguished by a tall neck with spreading mouth surmounted by a
simplified phoenix head. The peony scroll design was carved through
a white slip, the background being cut away and thus exposing the
reddish colour of the clay. The decorative band was then covered with
a green overglaze. The rest of the body is covered with a white slip
under a transparent white glaze. Although glazes with only two
colours, green and white, were used, a three-colour effect has been
achieved with the additional reddish colour of the body, showing
through at the shoulder.

CF. *Sekai Tōji Zenshū*, Vol. 10, Tokyo, 1955, Colour Pl. 19 (Museum
Yamato Bunka-kan).

80 VASE *(mei p'ing)*
*Liao Dynasty, 916-1124*
*Porcellaneous stoneware with black glaze  H. 17 3/4 in. (45.05 cm.)*
*926.21.93*

Slender, swelling body and contracted neck. Horizontal wheel rib-
bing. The *mei p'ing* shape became one of the most popular and distinctive shapes during the Sung Dynasty.

CF. *Sekai Tōji Zenshū*, Vol. 10, Tokyo, 1955, p. 250, Fig. 181.

82 VASE
*Yüan Dynasty, first half of 14th century*
*Ch'ing-pai ware* H. 11 3/16 in. (28.9 cm.) 922.20.98

Pear-shaped body. Carved decoration of dragon and waves above row
of stylized petals. Foliate pattern on neck. Details of waves and of
design on neck rendered in combed technique.

PUBL.: T. A. Heinrich, *Art Treasures in the Royal Ontario Museum,*
Toronto, 1963, p. 59.

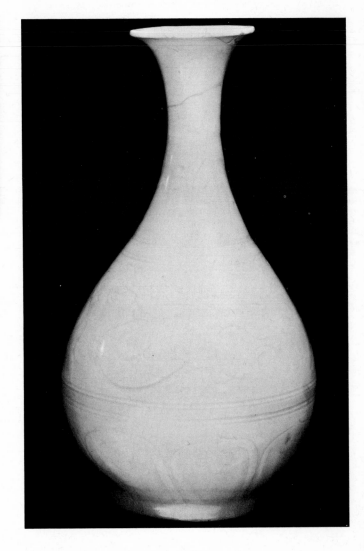

81 BOWL
*Ming Dynasty, early 15th century*
*Porcelain with incised and raised slip design* H. 4 in. (10.2 cm.); dia.
8 1/16 in. (20.5 cm.) 910.59.49

Inside, two rows of petals in raised slip design; outside, incised floral
scrolls below narrow key-fret border. Faintly bluish-white glaze.
Glazed, slightly convex base.

83 DISH
*Ming Dynasty, early 15th century*
*Porcelain decorated in underglaze blue   H. 2 3/4 in. (7 cm.); dia.*
*16 1/8 in. (41 cm.)  962.256*

In centre, bouquet of lotus, sagittaria and water chestnut tied with
fillet. Composite flower scroll in cavetto, border of stylized waves
below rim. Outside, composite flower scroll, bordered by key-fret
design round foot and scrolled band below rim. Unglazed base.

CF. J.A. Pope, *Chinese Porcelains from the Ardebil Shrine*, Washington, 1956, pl. 30; *Ming Blue-and-White*, The Museum of Far Eastern
Antiquities, Stockholm, 1964, No. 20.

84 JAR AND COVER
*Ming Dynasty, Interregnum, middle of 15th century*
*Porcelain decorated in underglaze blue    H. 13 1/2 in. (43.25 cm.)*
*925.25.15*

Centre section of jar has design of six large fruit sprays below sixfold
cloud collar framing floral sprays within its points which, in turn, fall
between floral sprays round body. Thick scroll band below. Unglazed
base burnt iron red in spots. Cover decorated with lotus scroll below
overlapping cloud collar motif enclosing floral forms round base of
knob. It is believed that the jar is slightly later than Hsüan-tê (1426-
35) and is therefore assigned to the Interregnum, between the end of
Hsüan-tê and the beginning of Ch'êng-hua (1465).

CF. J.A. Pope, *Chinese Porcelains from the Ardebil Shrine*, Washington, 1956, Pl. 52, No. 29.479.

PUBL.: Sir Harry M. Garner, *Oriental Blue and White*, London, 1954,
Pl. 23; *Tōjiki Zenshū* (Far Eastern Ceramics), Vol. II, Tokyo, 1959,
Pl. 33; A.M. Ferris, 'An Early Fifteenth Century Kuan in Toronto,'
*Oriental Art*, Summer, 1963, p. 98; T.A. Heinrich, *Art Treasures in the
Royal Ontario Museum*, Toronto, 1963, p. 67.

85 BOX AND COVER
*Ming Dynasty, six-character Chêng-tê mark and period (1506-21)*
*Porcelain decorated in underglaze blue* H. 4 1/4 in. (10.8 cm.); l.
10 1/4 in. (6.1 cm.); w. 6 1/8 in. (5.6 cm.) 925.25.2

Formal scrolls enclosing medallions with Arabic inscriptions. Trefoil
band round sides of cover. The two inscriptions may be translated
as 'Strive for excellence in penmanship, for it is one of the keys of
livelihood,' and 'A fool finds no contentment.'

CF. *Chinese Blue and White Porcelain*, The Oriental Ceramic Society,
London, 1954, No. 137.

PUBL.: 'West-East,' *R.O.M.A. Bulletin*, No. 21, Oct., 1953, No. 153; Sir
Harry M. Garner, *Oriental Blue and White*, London, 1954, Pl. 43 A
and text p. 28.

86 DEEP BOWL
*Ming Dynasty, late 16th century*
*Porcelain decorated in underglaze blue*    H. 7 1/16 in. (17.9 cm.); dia.
*13 in. (33 cm.)*    925.25.17

Broad band with ducks among lotus plants, flower sprays, willow
trees and rocks below scroll border. Flower sprays and cloud motifs
on wide rim. Unglazed base.

CF. *Sekai Tōji Zenshū*, Vol. 11, Tokyo, 1955, Pl. 118 (Wan-li mark and
period).

87 VASE of Kuan form
*Ming Dynasty, c. 1500*
*Porcelain with coloured glazes*   H. 13 3/8 in. (33.9 cm.)   939.35

Inner container and outer reticulated case, carved and covered with
aubergine, yellow and turquoise glazes. On body, broad band with
Taoist Immortals in landscape with pine trees, rocks, mountains and
clouds. Below, band of petals; above, floral scroll. Clouds round neck.

88 MODEL OF A RESIDENTIAL COMPOUND
*Ming Dynasty, 16th century*
*Pottery with green glaze  L. 6 ft., 10 in. (208 cm); w. 33 in. (83.8 cm.)  931.13.88-108*

Reddish ware with green glaze on roofs of buildings, walls and gates. Compound consists of three courtyards, with low pavilions and taller buildings joined by enclosing wall.

CF.. *Wên Wu*, 1959, No. 10, p. 19.

PUBL.: T. A. Heinrich, *Art Treasures in the Royal Ontario Museum*, Toronto, 1963, p. 65.

89 CYLINDRICAL BOX AND COVER
*Ming Dynasty, first half of 15th century*
*Lacquer H. 10 15/16 in. (27.8 cm.); dia. 11 1/2 in. (29.2 cm.)*
*952×8*

Red lacquer with deeply carved designs. Design of dragon pursuing pearl, surrounded by cloud scroll band, centred on cover. Sides of high cover decorated with dragons amid clouds in ogival medallions, separated by lotus scrolls. Plinth decorated with inverted lotus petal panels, diaper pattern containing eight-pointed flowers and open-work cloud-scroll motif. Interior covered with black lacquer.

PUBL.: *The Arts of the Ming Dynasty,* Detroit Institute of Art, No. 353; H. Trubner, 'Ming Lacquer in the Royal Ontario Museum,' *Annual,* ROM, 1962, Pls. XIII-XIV; T. A. Heinrich, *Art Treasures in the Royal Ontario Museum,* Toronto, 1963, p. 69.

72

91 JAR
*Transitional style, 17th century*
*Porcelain decorated in underglaze blue* H. 7 1/8 in. (18.1 cm.); dia.
at mouth 6 1/16 in. (15.4 cm.) 923.17.45

Broad band of figures in outdoor setting, mountains and swirling
clouds, characteristic of Transitional style. Band of descending leaves
below lip. Horizontal dividing lines bordering decorative motifs.
Unglazed, slightly concave base.

92 BOX AND COVER
*Ming Dynasty, middle of 16th century*
*Lacquer* H. 3 11/32 in. (8.4 cm.); dia. 7 1/2 in. 19 cm.) 961.201.1

Black *guri* lacquer with alternating layers of black and red. All-over
carved decoration of *ju-i* heads, arranged in a symmetrical pattern
and surrounding a central quatrefoil on cover.

CF. Sir Harry Garner, 'Guri Lacquer of the Ming Dynasty,' T.O.C.S.,
Vol. XXXI, 1957-59, Pl. 7 b.

PUBL.: H. Trubner, 'Ming Lacquer in the Royal Ontario Museum,'
*Annual*, ROM, 1962, Pl. XV; T. A. Heinrich, *Art Treasures in the Royal
Ontario Museum*, Toronto, 1963, p. 69.

90 SEATED FIGURE OF WÊN CH'ANG TI CHÜN, PATRON GOD OF LITERATURE
*Ming Dynasty, 16th century*
*Porcelain with coloured glazes* H. 32 3/8 in. (82.2 cm.); w. (of base)
14 1/2 in. (36.8 cm.) 918.21.581

Wên Ch'ang, in robes of state, seated on rectangular base. Green,
yellow, dark brown, turquoise and cream glazes. Both hands restored.

*Ch'ing Dynasty, late 17th or early 18th century*
*Porcelain decorated in underglaze blue   H. 17 1/6 in. (43.3 cm.)*
*923.17.56*

Design of tree, peony and magnolia, rocks, birds, insects and grasses.
Floral sprays on neck. Double ring in underglaze blue on base.

94 BRUSH POT
*Transitional style, 17th century*
*Porcelain decorated in underglaze blue   H. 7 3/8 in. (18.8 cm.);*
*dia. 8 3/16 in. (20.8 cm.)   908.6.6*

Broad band of figures in outdoor setting bordered by finely incised
horizontal lines and scroll band above, band with hatched design
below. Unglazed, slightly concave base.

74

95 SEATED FIGURE OF WÊN CH'ANG TI CHÜN, PATRON GOD OF LITERATURE
*Ch'ing Dynasty, 18th century*
*From Fukien, Tê-hua porcelain* H. 14 31/32 in. (38 cm.) 922.20.124

Square seal mark of potter Ho Chao-tsung impressed into clay on upper back. Figure wearing robes of state, seated on rocky base, left arm resting on ledge. Glossy grayish-white glaze.

CF. Ming example of same subject, with polychrome glazes, No. 90.

96 BALUSTER-SHAPED VASE
*Ch'ing Dynasty, K'ang-hsi period (1662-1722)*
*Porcelain decorated in underglaze blue and overglaze enamels* H. 16 5/8 in. (42.2 cm.) 911.4.32

Delicate enamels, of type known as *tou-ts'ai*, applied in second firing, over painting in underglaze blue. Body decorated with design of 'the three friends' (pine, prunus and bamboo). Moon rendered in iron red and soft underglaze blue outlines. Narrow borders with abstract designs, including key-fret band round exterior of lip and scroll band on splayed foot, complete the decoration. Underglaze blue Ch'êng-hua mark in three columns of two characters each, within double ring, on base.

The term *tou-ts'ai* is often mistranslated 'fighting colours' but no doubt refers to the second meaning of *tou* which is 'agreeable' or 'harmonious'. The use of *tou-ts'ai* enamels goes back to the Ch'êng-hua reign (1465-87) and can be observed on the familiar chicken cups and other enamelled porcelains of that period.

See caption 99 on page 78.

98 JAR
*Early Edo period, late 17th century*
*Kakiemon ware   H. 7 3/4 in. (19.7 cm.)   959.150*

Porcelain with delicately painted design of chrysanthemums, grasses and rockery in overglaze red, blue, green and yellow enamels. Petal design on shoulder and saw-tooth pattern round neck. Horizontal dividing lines painted in underglaze blue. The style of decoration is characteristic of early Kakiemon ware.

Kakiemon ware was made near Arita in Kyūshū and derives its name from that of an illustrious family of potters. The first Kakiemon is generally given credit for his contribution in developing, about the middle of the seventeenth century, the method of decorating porcelain with overglaze enamels. Red, green and an overglaze blue were the principal colours employed. The red enamel perfected by this potter resembled the colour of persimmon (*kaki*) and the name Kakiemon was thus adopted by him. It was subsequently applied to the name of the ware. A strong Chinese flavour is evident in the designs and brilliant colours of early Kakiemon, for they were inspired by the enameled porcelains of the K'ang-hsi period (1662-1722).

PUBL.: T. A. Heinrich, *Art Treasures in the Royal Ontario Museum*, Toronto, 1963, pp. 77; S. Jenyns, *Japanese Porcelain*, Faber and Faber, London, 1965, Pl. 54A ('Arita' ware).

OVERLEAF

97 SQUARE DISH
*Momoyama period, 1573-1615*
*E-Shino (Painted Shino) ware   H. 2 1/2 in. (6.4 cm.), l. and w. 6 3/8 in. (16.2 cm.)   964.84.2*

Heavy stoneware body of irregular shape, with rounded sides and high foot. Decorated with painted designs in iron brown, faintly tinged with pink, under thick, crackled white glaze. Foliate design centred inside and surrounded by band of abstract decoration. Outside, foliate sprays and grasses. Three low, knob-like supports on base.

Shino ware was greatly admired by devotees of the tea ceremony for its simple shapes and rich feldspathic glaze. It was made near Tajimi, in Gifu, an area renowed for its ceramic products.

Archaeological excavations carried out in Japan in recent years have brought to light rich finds of stone and pottery from the Jōmon period, some of them going back as far as the fifth millennium B.C., and extensive finds of a bronze and iron culture with strong ties to the East Asian mainland, whence it was introduced into Japan in the early centuries of the Christian era. The term *Jōmon*, commonly used for the period which is largely Neolithic, means 'cord pattern' and refers to the method of decorating pottery by impressions of twisted cord. Jōmon pottery consists primarily of vessels with abstract, often geometric decoration which seems purely decorative, rather than symbolic or representational. Cult images in the form of human figures, usually female, are also known and begin to appear after about the Middle Jōmon period (*c.* 3000-2000 B.C.).

The Jōmon period, which extended close to the end of the pre-Christian era, was succeeded by the relatively briefer Yayoi period, named after a place in Toyko where reddish pottery was first found during the last decades of the nineteenth century. Towards about 300 A.D. the Yayoi period was followed by the Protohistoric period, centred in the Yamato plain, south-east of Osaka. The Protohistoric period is remembered principally by the large number of tomb mounds raised over the graves of eminent personages, a practice derived from Korea, a country with which Japan had established close diplomatic relations. Most significant of all, from an artistic point, was the making of clay cylinders or *haniwa* which were placed close together to enclose the exterior of the mound like a fence. Many such *haniwa*, the tops of which were decorated with models of warriors, women, horses, dogs or monkeys, have come to light and are very much sought after for their simple beauty and lively animation. The *haniwa* represent an essentially indigenous culture, which continued until it was displaced in the sixth century by an entirely foreign element brought to Japan with the introduction of Buddhism.

The Japanese imperial house, following the founding of a new capital in Yamato, near Nara, maintained close contacts with the three Korean kingdoms of Koguryo, Paekche (Kudara, the southwest kingdom) and Silla, which were vying for control of the peninsula. In A.D. 538 the first Buddhist scriptures and images were brought to Japan from Kudara. The new religion soon gained a more secure foothold as the rulers of Yamato, swayed by the promise of protection for the realm and the Emperor, invited Korean monks and craftsmen to Japan to provide the objects required for the worship of the new religion. Immigrants from China were similarly welcomed.

Buddhism grew steadily in power and influence in Japan in the sixth century and flourished under the benevolent influence of the Empress Suiko (A.D. 593-628) and particularly her nephew and Regent, Shōtoku Taishi (A.D. 574-622), who was converted to Buddhism and actively encouraged the religion by his official patronage and support. Largely through his religious zeal the great temple of Hōryu-ji, a veritable storehouse of Buddhist art, was founded. The largest and most famous image in the temple, the gilt bronze Shaka Trinity which still forms the central image in the Kondo (Golden Hall), was dedicated in A.D. 623 in fulfilment of a vow made by Shōtoku. It is the work of Tori Busshi, descendant of a Chinese immigrant. The distinctive style of the Shaka Trinity, strongly influenced by the Buddhist art of the Northern Wei Dynasty (A.D. 386-535), is commonly referred to as the Tori style. Inherited by way of Korea, the style becomes highly individual in the hands of the Tori school of sculptors, and its characteristics can be observed in a number of Buddhist sculptures of the Asuka period (A.D. 538-645). The archaic smile, the emphasis upon large heads, hands and feet, and the symmetrical saw-tooth draperies are derived from Chinese prototypes, but expressed in a more personal manner and with an intensity which are clearly the mark of the Asuka period. Compared to their Chinese counterparts, the images of bronze and wood show a greater awareness of the plastic qualities of sculpture and communicate more directly with the worshipper as divine kings rather than as abstract entities. The beautiful bronze images were skilfully cast by the *cire perdue* method, and even in this early period the Japanese craftsmen distinguished themselves as great masters of the woodcarving technique.

China continued to exert a strong influence on the early culture of Japan. In the Nara period (A.D. 645-794) close diplomatic and cultural relations with T'ang China affected virtually every aspect of politics, religion and society in Japan. Despite the hazards of the voyage, Japanese travellers, including diplomats, monks, scholars, and craftsmen, were frequent visitors to Ch'ang-an, the T'ang capital, and returned to Japan deeply impressed with everything they saw, particularly with the beauty and richness of T'ang culture. In A.D. 710

the Japanese capital was moved to Nara, the street plan of which imitated the gridiron plan of Ch'ang-an. Even the administration of the Japanese government was revised, modelled upon that of China, thus strengthening the central power which came to extend its authority over most of the country.

Buddhism, now officially accepted, became all-powerful. Much of its popularity was due to the encouragement and support given by the Emperor Shōmu, a devout Buddhist who ordered a temple to be built in every province. The provincial temples were to be subordinate to the Tōdai-ji, the official temple at Nara, which housed the colossal bronze image, the Daibutsu, representing Vairocana. At the same time, Buddhist images of bronze, wood and the new media of dry lacquer (kanshitsu) or clay were produced in large quantities to fill the Tōdai-ji and other temples, greatly encouraging the development of Buddhist sculpture.

The accomplishment and richness of this sculpture can be seen in the many statues still preserved in the Tōdai-ji, Ya-kushi-ji, Kofuku-ji and other great temples of Nara. The influence of the T'ang style is very much in evidence, but the Japanese sculptors were able to impart to their work a more natural style, with a greater freedom of poses and more lifelike expressions, although the figures remain idealized and heroic. Very often the faces suggest a youthful spirit, but whether the expression is tranquil or ferocious, the features usually express great power and strong characterization.

Japanese art, when compared with its corresponding manifestations in China, always shows the marks of its own native tradition. This is true even in the eighth century, when the influence of T'ang China was considerable. Aside from stylistic differences, the Japanese artists invariably demonstrate a sensitivity for the material, particularly wood, so that the sweeping cuts of the carver's knife rendering drapery folds skilfully follow the grain of the wood and preserve the feeling of the log from which the statue was carved. While the statues of the Tempyō period are often more natural and lifelike than their T'ang counterparts, the Japanese soon developed their own formula of religious mysticism. The esoteric Shingon and Tendai sects founded by two famous priests, Kōbō Daishi and Dengyō Daishi, in the ninth century, introduced a fresh pantheon of deities and a complicated iconography which lent an entirely different cast to Japanese paint-

99 DISH
*Edo period, late 17th century*
*Iro-Nabeshima (Coloured Nabeshima) ware* H. 1 1/2 in. (3.9 cm.); dia. 6 1/8 in. (15.5 cm.) 959.149

Fine white porcelain, decorated inside with *sarasa* (textile) design derived from Persian textile pattern. Decoration of floral medallions and interlaced design, painted in underglaze blue, and red, green, and yellow enamels. Outside decorated with floral scrolls in underglaze blue above comb pattern round high foot, characteristic of Nabeshima ware.
Nabeshima ware was first made at Iwayagawachi, near Arita, then at Nangawara; about 1675 the kilns were moved to Okōchi. The Okōchi kilns remained in operation until the end of the Edo period, and most extant examples of Iro-Nabeshima are products of the Okōchi kilns in Hizen Province, Kyūshū. The kilns were established by the Lords of Nabeshima, rulers of Saga, and their production was strictly controlled by members of the clan. The ware was not exported, but was exclusively reserved for the clan's private use.

CF. *Iro-Nabeshima*, Heian-do, Kyoto, 1954, p. 114, Fig. 84; *Sekai Tōji Zenshū*, Vol. 4, Tokyo, 1956, p. 250, Fig. 189 (left column, centre); S. E. Lee, *Japanese Decorative Style*, The Cleveland Museum of Art, 1961. No. 151.

PUBL.: T. A. Heinrich, *Art Treasures in the Royal Ontario Museum*, Toronto, 1963, p. 77.

ing and sculpture. The art of the ninth and tenth centuries, inspired by the teachings of the Shingon and Tendai sects, is often distinguished by strangely austere, brooding figures with heavy bodies and mysterious expressions, and a complex, abstract form of painting known as a *mandara*. In place of the youthful, usually well-articulated figures of the preceding age, the Jōgan or Early Heian style tends to favour full-faced, bulky figures whose countenances radiate a deep spiritual calm, yet appear sombre and withdrawn.

In A.D. 794 the court had moved from Nara to the area of present-day Kyoto, the city of Tranquil Peace. The new capital, too, was constructed along Chinese lines, and T'ang influence continued to be felt until the tenth century, when formal diplomatic contacts with China were reduced and ultimately ceased altogether. The period of voluntary isolation lasted for three hundred years, during which time the nobility of Japan, which had long been guided by Chinese manners and customs, began to assume its own native character.

The Fujiwara clan, founded by Fujiwara-no-Kamatari, came to rule in the name of the Emperor, and the era from the ninth to the twelfth century is often referred to as the Fujiwara period. The Fujiwara family was not only a powerful political force, but also actively provided encouragement and support for the arts.

Not all the arts of the period were under the influence of the esoteric sects. Many court nobles preferred the Amida cult, and its simple path to salvation, to the elaborate ritual and complex iconography of the Shingon and Tendai sects. Under the influence of the Fujiwara clan, much of the Buddhist sculpture and painting gradually took on a lighter and more delicate character. A climax in this effort to bring the gods closer to man was reached with the designing and building in 1053 of the Hōōdo (Phoenix Hall) as the main hall of the Byōdo-in, near Kyoto. The Byōdo-in, originally the villa of Prime Minister Fujiwara-no-Michinaga (A.D. 966-1024), had been converted into a monastery in A.D. 1052. The name Hōōdo or Phoenix Hall is derived from the fact that its plan resembles a descending phoenix and thus symbolizes the concept of Paradise. The four surrounding walls were originally richly painted with scenes depicting the Pure Land, the Paradise of Amida. A frieze of fifty-one wood carvings of heavenly beings and of monks floating on clouds, placed around the upper part of the walls, completed the suggestion of a heavenly Paradise. The Phoenix Hall still houses the famous wood,

lacquered and gilt image of Amida, a celebrated work by the sculptor Jōchō. The large image of Amida and the paintings and reliefs on the side walls clearly represent an attempt to personalize the deity and to bring the idea of Paradise within the reach of everyone, for rebirth in the Paradise of Amida was now open to all who invoked his name.

The very fine wood image of Jizō in the museum's collection, from the first half of the tenth century, also communicates the idea of salvation and divine mercy (Pl. 100). The delicate carving and gentle face express the benign nature of Jizō, one of the principal Buddhist deities of mercy, and the saviour of those condemned to suffering in the underworld. The statue is carved from a solid block of wood in the *ichiboku* (single block) technique. This method of carving from a single block was gradually replaced by the *yosegi* (joined block) technique. Jōchō, the sculptor of the celebrated Amida in the Hōōdo, is traditionally regarded as the originator of the *yosegi* technique.

A painted version of Amida's Western Paradise is represented by the Taima Mandara, a major example of Buddhist painting of the Kamakura period (Pl. 104). It is attributed to the second half of the thirteenth century. The elaborate composition with pavilions and terraces depicts on the upper levels Bodhisattvas and other heavenly beings accompanying the central figure of Amida, a sacred pond with boats, mandarin ducks and tiny figures floating on lotus blossoms. In the foreground a group of musicians and dancers perform on a terrace. The various components of the composition all convey the concept of Paradise, a land of bliss and happiness. The spirit of the painting contrasts sharply with the introspective and meditative attitudes of Buddhism predominant in the sculpture and painting of the ninth and tenth centuries.

The Taima Mandara, although a product of the Kamakura period, derives from a famous composition in tapestry, representing the Paradise of Amida, which dates from the second half of the eighth century and belongs to the Taima-dera temple. It thus represents a traditional subject while preserving something of the enlightened spirit of the Fujiwara age. The art of the Kamakura period usually expresses more strongly the martial spirit of the new military government (*bakufu*) set up at Kamakura in A.D. 1185 by Minamoto-no-Yoritomo, a famous military figure, after his victory over the rival Taira clan. This event put a formal end to the Fujiwara era and the aristocratic, refined life of the court at Kyoto. In the arts of the Kamakura period a new vigour and intensity generally replaced the elegance and restraint of the preceding age. The wood sculpture, in particular, showed great power and dramatic intensity, often combined with strong realism and an interest in surface detail. Buddhist painting became more direct and emotional, full of dramatic movement and asymmetric in composition. Portraiture, which lent itself particularly well to the new realism, reached new heights of expression. A fresh interest in heroic action and adventure brought about the florescence of narrative scroll paintings – long horizontal scrolls depicting various themes drawn from national history, from legends relating to various Buddhist temples, from the biographies of famous monks, and many other subjects. It is in the field of narrative scrolls that Japanese art has made one of its most original and most enduring contributions.

With the fall of the Kamakura military government, civil strife once more disrupted Japan's internal peace. This period, commonly known as Namboku-chō, ended with the ultimate victory of the Ashikagas, whose leader ruled in the name of the Emperor and assumed the title of Shogun. The Ashikagas, who were now the real power behind the throne, were enlightened rulers who continued the policy of active encouragement and support of the arts. They lived in the Muromachi district of Kyoto, hence the name, Muromachi, commonly given to the period from A.D. 1334 to 1573. The Ashikaga rulers also built elegant villas, such as the Kinkaku-ji (Golden Pavilion) and Ginkaku-ji (Silver Pavilion), which were to serve as places for retirement and relaxation, where such fashionable pastimes as the tea ceremony would be practised.

One of the most significant developments of the Muromachi age was the rising popularity of the Zen sect of Buddhism. As opposed to the complex iconography and meditative practices of other sects, Zen emphasized contemplation and austerity in order to attain Buddhahood, which was believed to lie dormant within every individual, requiring only to be aroused. The directness and simplicity of Zen, seeking peace and harmony with nature, appealed to the Shoguns and their way of life and had a profound effect upon Japanese civilization. The unaffected, contemplative nature of Zen strongly influenced the designs of Japanese gardens and was largely responsible for the austerity of the objects and settings associated with the tea ceremony. In painting, Zen resulted

in the great popularity of pure ink painting (*sumi-e*), derived from Chinese painting of the Southern Sung Dynasty (A.D. 1127-1279). The swiftly drawn, abbreviated designs which distinguish Zen painting, and reflect the abstract nature of Zen teaching, greatly appealed to the Ashikaga rulers. The collection's hanging scroll of Gibbons (959.51) is an excellent and typical example of sixteenth century Zen painting. The economy of taste and simplicity of means expressed in such paintings are also reflected in the ceramics and other utensils of the period made specifically for use in the tea ceremony.

During the brief Momoyama period (A.D. 1573-1615) powerful feudal lords succeeded one another as rulers of Japan and as patrons of the arts. Three famous warriors, Oda Nobunaga (A.D. 1534-1582), who displaced the last Ashikaga Shogun, and his successors Toyotomi Hideyoshi (A.D. 1536-1598) and Tokugawa Ieyasu (A.D. 1542-1616) built great castles, symbols of their military power, and vied in their patronage of the arts. The interiors of the massive and dimly lit stone castles were elaborately decorated with lavish screens and paintings in rich colours, often on grounds of gold or silver, with brightly gilded wood carvings in adjoining panels and partitions. Compared to the austerity of Zen taste, which dominated the arts of the Muromachi period, the arts of the Momoyama and succeeding Edo period (A.D. 1615-1868) emphasized the opulence and gorgeousness of the decorative designs. Only in tea ceremony ceramics were simplicity and restraint still the rule. Provincial wares such as Oribe, Seto and Shino were adapted by the tea masters to conform to the humble requirements of the tea ceremony. The restrained patterns which distinguish these wares show the creative capacity and unusual skill of the Momoyama potters.

The collection has two excellent examples of Momoyama tea ceremony ceramics: a square Dish of Shino ware, decorated with painted designs in iron brown under a typical, thick Shino glaze (Pl. 97), and a recently acquired Dish of Oribe ware. Shino and Oribe are two of the most famous types of Momoyama pottery made specifically for use in the tea ceremony. The two examples, which are typical of their respective wares, are distinguished by their simplicity and bold, abstract designs, qualities which are in harmony with the purity of Zen and the austerity of the tea ceremony.

The Edo period was established in A.D. 1615, when Tokugawa Ieyasu triumphed over his rivals and set himself up as Shogun to consolidate his power. The period takes its name

100 JIZŌ BOSATSU (*Sanskrit:* Ksitigarbha)
*Heian period, first half of 10th century*
*Wood with traces of pigment   H. 41 1/16 in. (104.3 cm.)   960.83*

Jizō Bosatsu is a Buddhist saviour, residing in the Buddha-less world which extends from the nirvana (extinction of self, i.e. death) of Shaka (Śākyamuni) to the advent of Miroku (Maitreya, the Buddhist Messiah). He is often worshipped as Emmyō (life-prolonging) Jizō, for he is believed to lead men to piety, eliminate all suffering and lengthen life. He is also worshipped as a patron saint of children, who guides them away from the bed of the under-world river where they are wandering.

The figure is reported to have come from Kofuku temple, Nara. It is an example of the *ichiboku* (single block) technique of wood carving commonly employed from the seventh to the eleventh century. The head and body of the figure were carved from a single block of wood, the hands alone being added separately. This method was gradually superseded in the eleventh century by the *yosegi* (joined block) technique. The style of the figure, particularly the treatment of the drapery folds descending in sweeping curves over the legs, still reflects some of the characteristic features of the earlier Jōgan period.

CF. *The Evolution of the Buddha Image*, the Asia Society Inc., New York, 1963, No. 57 (Torso of Buddha from Toshodai-ji, Nara, ninth century).

PUBL.: *Archives*, Vol. XIV, 1960, p. 77, Fig. 37; T. A. Heinrich, *Art Treasures in The Royal Ontario Museum*, Toronto, 1963, p. 73.

from the new capital set up in the village of Edo (present-day Tokyo) in order to escape the effete influence of the former court at Kyoto. Edo rapidly rose to become the political, economic and cultural centre of Japan, although Kyoto still retained its position as the country's foremost artistic centre. The Edo period represents a new era of political stability and external peace, centred around the enlightened rule of the Tokugawa Shoguns. In art, the new styles which were introduced generally continued the essentially decorative trend of the Momoyama period. The Shoguns and the Kyoto court supported the official Kanō and Tosa schools of painting, which represent a continuation of the academic manner. Meanwhile a new school of popular art, known as *Ukiyo-e*, came to flourish in the commercial centres of Edo and Osaka, where a new and prosperous merchant class came to prominence during the extended period of peace encouraged by the firm rule of the Shoguns. Although townspeople were at the bottom of the social hierarchy, their influence as patrons of the arts grew as their wealth and power increased. The merchants enjoyed genre painting and the art of *Ukiyo-e*, popularized in wood-block prints and paintings which depicted such themes as the *kabuki* and the gay quarter. The Shoguns, on the other hand, supported the artists of the Kanō school, representative of 'official' taste, but the accomplishments of the Kanō artists became gradually more and more academic and sterile.

The pair of six-fold screens of Flower Carts, painted in ink and colours on gold-leafed paper, are representative of the Kanō school and reflect an interest in Japan's classical tradition (Pl. 108). The screens of Chickens and Plum Trees, by Itō Jakuchū, are examples of the realistic style of painting which was developed in Kyoto during the eighteenth century (Pl. 107). Jakuchū, who specialized in the painting of chickens, was one of the foremost exponents of this style.

The decorative arts also flourished during the Edo period, and beautifully potted wares for the tea ceremony as well as high-fired porcelains were produced in large numbers.

Pottery for the tea ceremony, as illustrated by the Raku bowl (Pl. 103), consisted of simple shapes, with subtle glazes and sparse designs. The manufacture of porcelain, introduced into Japan early in the seventeenth century with the discovery of porcelain clay at Izumiyama, near Arita, developed rapidly. Although sometimes inspired by Chinese and Korean prototypes, Japanese potters were soon able to produce high-fired porcelains decorated with brilliant enamel designs. The technique of decorating porcelain in overglaze enamels was introduced and perfected by the Kakiemon family, and a very fine example of early Kakiemon ware, showing the beginning of the enamelling technique in Japan, is represented by the late seventeenth century porcelain jar, with decoration in polychrome enamels (Pl. 98). In Japan, pieces of this type are usually referred to as 'Kakiemon I' in accordance with the traditional view that about the middle of the seventeenth century Kakiemon I, with the help of Tokuyemon, an Arita pottery merchant, was the first to develop the technique of overglaze enamelling on porcelain.

The shallow dish with high foot and decoration of *sarasa* or textile pattern painted in underglaze blue and red, green and yellow enamels, is typical of Nabeshima ware, another important type of Early Edo poreclain (Pl. 99). Nabeshima, which from a technical viewpoint is the most refined and perfect of Japanese porcelains, was made for the exclusive use of the Lords of Nabeshima, rulers of Saga Prefecture, in Kyusho. Compared to Kakiemon, the designs on Nabeshima porcelain are often more subtle and delicate, and the colours more refined.

The Edo period also saw the ultimate development of Japanese costume and textile design and the production of richly patterned gowns decorated in brilliant colours. The museum has many fine examples of textiles from the Edo period, illustrating various types and techniques. Some of these were derived from Chinese and European techniques, introduced in the Momoyama period, while others, such as *yuzen* dyeing, were newly invented in the Edo period.

101 HEAD OF JŪICHIMEN KANNON
*Heian period, late 10th or 11th century*
*Wood   H. 13 1/4 in. (33.6 cm.)   Gift of Mrs. Edgar J. Stone, 960.260.1*

Originally part of a statue of Jūichimen Kannon (Eleven-headed
Kannon; Sanskrit: *Ekadasamukha*), one of the 'Six Forms of Kannon'
and a manifestation of Avalokiteśvara (Chinese: *Kuan-yin*). Jūichimen Kannon is usually represented as having eleven diminutive
heads in addition to the main one, ten symbolizing the several
courses leading to enlightenment and one symbolizing the resultant
final attainment of enlightenment. The three diminutive heads on
the front of Jūichimen Kannon ordinarily show mercy, three on the
left show anger, three on the right show ferocious expressions with
fangs projecting upward (as in the present head); one on the back
shows a laughing face and the one at the very top shows the face
of the Buddha.
The small seated figure in the crown on the Museum's head represents Amida, spiritual father of Kannon. In the Early Heian period,
during the Kōnin (810-823) and Jōgan (859-876) eras, esoteric Buddhism became immensely popular and resulted in highly stylized,
mystical representations of Buddhist divinities, such as Jūichimen
Kannon.

CF. *The Evolution of the Buddha Image*, The Asia Society, Inc., New
York, 1963, No. 55.

102 SHINTO GODDESS
*Heian period, 12th century*
*Cryptomeria wood   H. 38 in. (96.5 cm.)   957.228*

Standing figure, carved in *ichiboku* technique. Flat from front to back and intended to be viewed from front. Details of carving generally confined to front. Upright, symmetrical pose with hands folded in front and hidden inside sleeves.

The figure forms part of a set of twelve Shinto deities, sometimes believed to have come from the Izu peninsula, southwest of Tokyo, or from Izumo Province, on the northwest coast of the main island of Japan. Other examples of this group are in the Cleveland Museum, the Art Institute of Chicago, in the collection of Bradley Martin (on loan to the Brooklyn Museum), the Honolulu Academy of Arts, and in a private collection in Japan.

Examples of Shinto sculpture are exceedingly rare because of the reluctance to portray Shinto gods as humans. They were initially regarded as spirits, too mysterious to recreate in plastic or pictorial form. The practice of making sacred images for the Shinto shrines did not arise until the beginning of the Early Heian period (ninth century), when it was adopted from the popular Buddhist custom of worshipping images set up in temples. Shinto deities were generally regarded as mythical ancestors of the Japanese and are therefore represented as humans, wearing the costumes of the various periods in which they were made.

CF. S. E. Lee, 'A Hand and an Image of Wood,' *Bulletin, Cleveland Museum of Art*, Vol. XLIV, Jan. 1957, pp. 6-9; Jack Sewell, 'Four Newly Acquired Examples of Japanese Art,' *The Art Institute of Chicago Quarterly*, Vol. LII, No. 1, pp. 10-16, Feb. 1958.

PUBL.: *Annual*, Art and Archaeology Division, ROM, 1959, p. 56, Pl. XIV.

103 TEA BOWL
*Edo Period, 18th century*
*Raku ware  H. 3 5/8 in. (9.3 cm.); dia. of mouth 4 in. (10.3 cm.)*
944.16.4

Decorated in style of Kōrin – Koetsu decorative school of painting. Lustrous black glaze with crane reserved in white on outside, a turtle inside.

Raku was developed in Kyoto, from the second half of the sixteenth century and was highly prized as a ware designed exclusively for use in the tea ceremony. Bowls by the first Raku, Chōjirō, and by Dōnyu, the third, are the most famous. The bright lustre of the black glaze and thick flow are distinguishing features of the ware.

PUBL.: S. E. Lee, *Japanese Decorative Style*, Cleveland Museum of Art, 1961, No. 137.

OPPOSITE

104 TAIMA MANDARA
*Kamakura period, second half of 13th century*
*Hanging scroll in full colour and gold on silk; the gold applied in*
*kirikane (cut-gold) technique  H. 73 1/8 in. (185.5 cm.); w. 62 5/8*
*in. (159.5 cm.)  959.118*

A symmetrical composition and highly decorative treatment characterize the painting. At the centre, Amida Buddha, Lord of the Western Paradise of bliss and supreme happiness, is seated on a lotus throne beneath an elaborate canopy, accompanied by his two principal Bodhisattvas, Seishi and Kannon, a host of other Bodhisattvas, musicians and heavenly beings. In front there are terraces surrounding the sacred pond, flanked by a holy tree to the left and right. Behind and above Amida there are terraces and pavilions; celestial beings can be seen on the terraces, in the pavilions and in the sky above. The central composition of Amida's paradise as well as the borders illustrate the text of the *Kanmuryōju-kyō* (the sutra on the meditation of Buddha Amitayus, and Queen Vaidehi's persecution by Prince Ajatasatru). In the left and right borders various events are represented, corresponding to the text of the sutra.

The Taima Mandara presents a change from the metaphysical and meditative practices of the Shingon and Tendai sects, which flourished in the Jōgan period, in the ninth century, towards an enlightened attitude regarding Buddhism, developed in the Heian and Kamakura periods. Paintings of Amida's paradise, expressing the ideas of the Jōdo sect, suggest a feeling of proximity and intimacy between our world and Amida's land of bliss. They brought the concept of Paradise visibly closer and made possible the belief in a happy after-life.

In the present painting cut-gold leaf has been applied, notably in the patterns of the garments, a technique known as *kirikane*, which became popular during the Heian and Kamakura periods. The technique effectively emphasizes the minuteness of detail and reinforces the delicacy of the decorative patterns.

Besides an early sixteenth century copy at Taima-dera, there are several other representations of the Taima Mandara from the Kamakura period: in the Komyō-ji in Kamakura, Jōren-ji in Akita, Chion-in in Kyoto and in the collection of the Tokyo National Museum.

CF. S. Taki, 'On the Taima Mandara Painting,' *Kokka*, No. 247, 1910, pp. 159-170; No. 249, 1911, pp. 229-243; No. 251, 1911, pp. 287-297; see also p. 315 and Pl. VII (original Taima Mandara in Taima-dera); *Nihon Kokukō Zenshū* (National Treasures of Japan), Tokyo, 1923, Vol. 10, Pl. 191, Vol. 32, Pl. 629.

PUBL.: *Archives*, Vol. XIII, 1959, p. 100, Fig. 34; H. Trubner, 'Two Japanese Paintings,' *Annual*, Art and Archaeology Division, ROM, Toronto, 1960, pp. 46-47, Pl. XVII; T. A. Heinrich, *Art Treasures in the Royal Ontario Museum*, Toronto, 1963, p. 75.

105 BOWL
*Edo period, first half of 18th century*
*Ko-Imari (Old Imari) ware* H. 2 5/16 in. (5.9 cm.); dia. 5 1/6 in.
(12.9 cm.) 961.73

Porcelain, decorated in underglaze blue and overglaze red, green,
yellow enamels and gold. *Kylin* within double circle in underglaze
blue centred inside, surrounded by enamelled 'red jewel' design,
interspaced with pendants and chrysanthemum flowers. Below rim,
narrow border with floral and chevron pattern. Outside, tree-peony
and arabesque pattern in gold on dark blue ground; details scratched
through gold. Six-character mark 'Rarity like Jewel and Treasure' in
underglaze blue within double ring on base.

The prototype for this type of bowl, with enamelled and gilded

decoration combined with underglaze blue, is found in Chinese
enamelled wares of the Chia-ching period (1522-66).

Imari porcelains were widely exported to Europe during the
seventeenth and eighteenth centuries and take their name from the
port of Imari, near Arita, from which they were shipped. They
differed from early Kakiemon in their more elaborate designs, the
general use of underglaze blue and the appearance of a darker red
enamel.

CF. *Ko-Imari*, Kyoto, 1959, Colour Pl. 19.

PUBL.: *An Illustration of Japanese Coloured Porcelain*, Kyoto, 1958,
Pl. 98; Fujio Koyama, *Japanese Ceramics*, Oakland Art Museum, 1961,
No. 60; T. A. Heinrich, *Art Treasures in the Royal Ontario Museum*,
Toronto, 1963, p. 77.

106 SMALL BOX AND COVER
*Edo period, 18th century*
*Wood with gold lacquer* makie *(sprinkled picture)* H. 2 1/2 in.
*(6.4 cm.); l. 2 5/8 in. (6.7 cm.); w. 2 1/4 in. (5.8 cm.)   927.32.6 a-b*

Small, squarish box and cover, decorated with design of *nadeshiko*
(Chinese pink-flower) and grasses. Small rings attached to metal
fittings on two sides. The decoration is done in *kakiwari* (literally,
*remaining lines*). The designs were first drawn in gold over the

brown lacquer ground. Then gold and silver dust were sprinkled on
the ground, leaving the lines clear so that they stand out distinctly
from those portions covered with sprinkled gold. To separate the
petals, the *hari-bori* (needle carving) technique was used, whereby
the designs were scratched with a needle after sprinkling with gold
dust. The overall effect of these combined techniques is flat and for
this reason the decoration is referred to by the term *hira-makie*
(flat *makie*). The technique became very popular during the Momoyama and Edo periods.

**107** CHICKENS AND PLUM TREES
*By Itō Jakuchū (1716-1800)  Edo period, 18th century*
*Pair of six-fold screens in sumi on paper  H. (each screen) 68 1/2 in.*
*(174 cm.); w. 147 3/4 in. (375.2 cm.)  H. (each painting) 54 in.*
*(137.1 cm.); w. 21 in. (53.3 cm.)  965.63*

Itō Jakuchū was a prominent exponent of the realistic style of painting which was developed in Kyoto in the eighteenth century. He
first studied the work of the Kanō school, but subsequently became
very interested in Yüan and Ming bird-and-flower painting. The artist
grew up in Nishiki-no-Kōji, a street crowded with grocery shops and

fish markets, and found inspiration for his paintings among these
humble surroundings. His favourite subjects were chickens, which
he kept in his backyard and was thus able to study with great care.
The screens are distinguished by the simple, almost abstract character
of the individual compositions and careful observation of nature.
The brushwork is free and remarkably fluid, the effectiveness of the
painting depending on the strong handling of the brush, with
deliberate use of heavy accents of black ink against the white paper
and occasionally sweeping or broken strokes of the brush to heighten
the pictoral effects. Jakuchū has succeeded to a remarkable degree
in depicting the character and nature of chickens in these screens.

一株古梅如玉
條素三選色曉
詩歸

白山畫

Detail of 107. See preceding page.

OPPOSITE

**108 FLOWER CARTS**
*Edo period, 18th century*

*Pair of six-fold screens in full colour and gold on paper  H. 67 1/4 in. (170.7 cm.)  936.6.1*

Pair of screens with design of five carts, carrying seasonal flowers of spring and autumn respectively. Top screen, representing spring, shows three carts, one of which (on the far left) is decorated with design of cherry blossoms. The flowers shown in this screen are, from left to right, lilies, chrysanthemums, daffodils and, in the third cart, camellias. The lower screen, representing autumn, has two carts, one of which is decorated with a chrysanthemum pattern. The flowers in the carts are peonies, poppies, wistaria and bush clover. All but one of the carts have their carriages and wheels decorated with stylized vegetable and floral designs; the fifth cart is plain.
The screens clearly reflect the trend of the period when interest in the imperial court and in Japan's classical culture, centring around the court and nobility, was revived. The carts shown in the screens suggest the elegant court life of the Heian period, particularly the refinement and sophistication fostered by the Fujiwara court, when the Imperial family and noblemen used richly decorated carts pulled by bulls. The emphasis upon the beauty of the flowers also reflects the enlightened and creative spirit of the Fujiwara nobility. A similar subject was depicted in Sōtatsu's famous screen, called Sekiya, depicting a story from the Genji Monogatari.

CF. *Kokka*, No. 369, 1921, Pl. v, Flower cart painted on *sugido* (wooden sliding door) in Shōrakuden of Nagoya Palace, Nagoya.

109  WINE CUP AND STAND
*Korea, Koryŏ Dynasty, 12th – 13th century*
*Celadon ware  H. 5 1/4 in. (13.3 cm.)  924.30.1 a and b*

Foliate scrolls and formal chrysanthemums incised and filled with white and black slips under celadon glaze. Cup is ten-lobed and lip has scalloped edge. Cup supported on high stand having an everted rim with ten lobes and scalloped feet. Each lobe of cup and rim of stand decorated with chrysanthemum spray with white flowers and black leaves. Incised scroll band below scalloped edge of cup. Each lobe of interior and bottom of cup inside has incised chrysanthemum spray.

Towards centre of stand, in depressed portion, is incised foliate design, and each lobe of foot has incised floral spray. Carved pattern of overlapping petals encircles base of low dome which supports cup. Flat centre, surrounded by a raised rim, decorated with incised floral spray.

CF. *Masterpieces of Korean Art*, An exhibition under the Auspices of The Government of the Republic of Korea, 1957, No. 113.

# India

About 2300 B.C. a highly advanced culture was centred in the Indus Valley of north-west India (present-day Pakistan) at Mohenjo-daro and Harappa. This culture produced some of the most advanced city planning of the time, as shown by the gridiron layout of Mohenjo-daro with the principal avenues running north to south; it was also responsible for the earliest examples of Indian sculpture. Among the finds from Mohenjo-daro are a steatite male bust, perhaps representing a priest, with strong Mesopotamian influence, and a small copper figurine of a dancing girl, which already suggests some of the characteristics of later Indian sculpture.

The Indus Valley civilization flourished for some 600 years, until about 1700 B.C. Its end about 1500 B.C. was brought about by a combination of factors, probably the most important being the gradual desiccation of the region of Sind and the invasions of the Aryans, nomads from the Iranian Plateau or the Caspian Sea, who were pushing into India by the Khyber Pass. The upheavals which accompanied the Aryan conquest, from about 1500-1200 B.C., forced the Dravidian inhabitants of the Indus Valley to move south into the Deccan. The Indus Valley culture was at this time superseded by the age of the *Vedas*, the sacred books concerned with the performance of Brahmanic ritual, introduced by the Aryan conquerors. In contrast to Dravidian beliefs, centred around the worship of specific deities represented by images set up in shrines, the Vedic tradition stressed the worship of the powers of heaven and earth by hymns and sacrifices, without the use of temples or idols. The Aryans also introduced a host of deities, such as Indra, god of the atmosphere and thunder, and Sūrya, a solar god, corresponding to Apollo of the Hellenic tradition. The Aryan deities were later modified and combined with the Dravidian nature spirits, and were ultimately absorbed into the religious system known as Hinduism.

Of infinitely greater significance for the history of ancient Indian art, and having a far-reaching impact upon all the civilizations of Asia, was the rise of Buddhism and Buddhist art in the wake of Alexander the Great's conquest of north-west India early in the fourth century B.C. While Alexander's conquest was short-lived, the eastward march of his armies opened India to the Hellenic and Iranian civilizations of the west. The Maurya Dynasty, established the year after Alexander's death by Chandragupta Maurya, an ally of Alexander, maintained close diplomatic and cultural relations with the

OVERLEAF

110 CHAKRAPURUSA (Personification of Vishnu's discus)
*Kashmir, c. 600*
*Bronze   H. 9 1/2 in. (24.1 cm.)   939.17.21*

Probably part of larger Vishnu icon. Similar figure of Chakrapurusa appears as one of attendant figures of a Vishnu bronze image in Berlin.

CF. H. Hartel, 'Zur Datierung einer alten Visnu-Bronze,' *Indologen Tagung*, Göttingen, 1959, pp. 176-177, Fig. 59.

PUBL.: S. E. Lee, 'A Bronze Yaksha Image and its Significance,' *R.O.M.A. Bulletin*, No. 24, Dec., 1956, pp. 23-25; *Master Bronzes of India*, The Art Institute of Chicago, 1965, No. 13.

111 COLOSSAL HEAD OF BODHISATTVA
*Gandhāra, 4th – 5th century*
*Stucco H. 29 in. (73.6 cm.) Gift of Dr. C. T. Currelly in memory of Mary Treble Currelly, 939.19.1*

The head shows a combination of Late Classical naturalism, suggested by the modelling of the mouth, and oriental formalism as seen in the sharp linear definition of the eyes and brows. It thus illustrates the hybrid character of Gandhāra art.

PUBL.: 'West-East,' *R.O.M.A. Bulletin*, No. 21, Oct., 1953, No. 99; T. A. Heinrich, *Art Treasures in the Royal Ontario Museum*, Toronto, 1963, p. 81.

ancient kingdom of Bactria, an area centred around the modern city of Balkh, in modern Afghanistan, and a stronghold of Hellenic culture. The Bactrian kingdom in turn maintained close contacts with the Mediterranean world and served as an important cultural link between the ancient world and north-western India, particularly the kingdom of Gandhāra, occupying the area of modern Afghanistan. The Gandhāra kingdom formed part of the Kushan empire whose capital was at Mathurā (modern Muttra). From about the first to the fifth century the Gandhāra region witnessed the florescence of an important school of Buddhist architecture, sculpture and painting, Indian in content and iconography, but from a stylistic and artistic point of view strongly influenced by western art forms of Hellenistic and Roman origin.

In the earliest manifestations of Indian Buddhist art of the Maurya (322-185 B.C.) and Śunga (185-72 B.C.) Dynasties, centred around the miracles and events in the life of the historical Buddha, Śākyamuni (563-483 B.C.), the Buddha is never shown in human form. His presence, when indicated, is merely suggested by an appropriate symbol. Thus the relief carvings from the late Śunga stupa at Bhārut and other contemporary monuments of Buddhist art, and the somewhat later carvings from the gateways of the Great Stupa at Sāñchi, of Early Āndhra date, never feature the Buddha in anthropomorphic form. Instead, the artisans engaged in the decoration of these monuments employed various symbols, such as the wheel (the Wheel of the Law, set in motion by the Buddha when he preached the Sermon in the Deer Park at Sārnāth), the Bhodi Tree (beneath which he was seated when he received Enlightenment), an empty throne, or the riderless horse. The sculptors also made use of various allegorical references to the Buddha, suggested for example by the presence of the ancient Vedic deities, Sūrya and Indra, in the stone reliefs of the Buddhist *Vihara* (monastery) at Bhājā, southeast of Bombay, of the first century B.C.

Not until after the establishment of the Kushan Dynasty about the middle of the first century A.D., and the subsequent rise of a school of sculpture in the Gandhāra region, was the image of the Buddha in human form at last introduced. The Gandhāra school, which flourished in north-western India and Afghanistan from the first to the fifth centuries A.D., also appears to have originated the seated Buddha and the Bodhisattva type. It was, in addition, responsible for the codification of Buddhist iconography and the representation of the

Buddha legend in countless reliefs, made mostly to decorate the large number of stupas and Buddhist monasteries which were raised in this region. In these reliefs, the various episodes are no longer told according to the principle of the continuous narrative, a characteristic of the work from the earliest periods of Buddhist art, as illustrated by the carvings from Bhārhut and Sānchi. Instead, events from the Buddha legend are now related in a series of separate episodes. This new formula corresponds to the accepted Roman method of portraying events from the life of the emperors by a series of separate panels, each devoted to a single climactic incident.

The hybrid character of Gandhāra art, marked by strong influence from the West, represents an eastward extension of the art of the Roman empire, especially in its late and provincial manifestations, and an attempt to adapt this art to the spiritual requirements of Indian Buddhism. These influences from Asia Minor and the Roman world were undoubtedly transmitted to north-west India by journeying craftsmen, familiar with Roman art but not with the deeper meaning and iconography of Buddhist art. The result is a curious blending of Western and native Indian elements in the art of the Gandhāra school.

The essentially foreign nature of the Gandhāra phase of Indian art is well illustrated by the holdings of Gandhāra sculpture in the Museum collection, in the form of both large statues and reliefs. The products of the Gandhāra school are, as a rule, easily recognized by the use of a dark bluish-gray schist or green phyllite, commonly employed for carving in the Peshawar Valley and the Taxila region during the early centuries of the Christian era.

The standing image of a Bodhisattva (Pl. 112), clad in *dhoti* and shawl, and wearing an amulet box suspended from a chain, necklaces and other jewelry, is typical of the Bodhisattva type produced in the Gandhāra workshops. This image and other similar representations can probably be regarded as portrayals of Prince Siddharta prior to his enlightenment, wearing the princely garments of a contemporary rajah. The Gandhāra Buddhas and images of many of the lesser deities, often clad in heavy Roman togas rather than the Buddhist *sanghātī* (monastic robe), are distinguished by youthful, often effeminate features and wavy hair, recalling the style of the Apollo Belvedere, while the poses show a *déhanchement* of the body evidently derived from the Praxitelean treatment of the human figure. The collection also contains an interest-

ing group of Gandhāra reliefs, some of which depict famous incidents from the legend of the Buddha in a rather crowded late Roman style. Others, particularly the stair-riser reliefs from Buddhist stupas and monasteries, frequently depict drinking scenes or other scenes of merriment, with male and female figures sometimes arranged on a single plane and isolated against a plain background, in a style which is distinctly classical and recalls Roman work of the Augustan age (Pl. 113). The chiton and himation as well as the Indian *dhoti* and shawl occur, and illustrate the curious mixture of classical and Indian elements in Gandhāra art. Of unusual interest is the relief with male figures in Iranian costume and carrying swords, inspired by the influx of yet another foreign influence upon the hybrid art of north-west India (Pl. 114).

After the middle of the third century the use of stone declined and stucco or lime plaster, only sparsely used in the early phase of Gandhāra art, replaced it in the decoration of Buddhist architecture. Stucco had been widely employed in Iran as a form of architectural revetment, and it is quite possible that its widespread use in late Gandhāra art was the result of fresh contacts with Iran in the wake of the Sassanian invasion of Shapur I in A.D. 241. The impressive large stucco Head (Pl. 111), once part of a statue of evidently enormous proportions, is a particularly fine example of the last phase of Gandhāra sculpture, when stucco was in almost universal use. The stucco heads, surviving in large numbers from sites in Afghanistan and the Peshawar Valley, were usually attached to bodies made of mud covered by only a thin outer layer of lime-plaster, with the result that the bodies have all long since disintegrated.

The humanistic art of Gandhāra, derived from Western concepts, was incompatible with the spiritual and mystical nature of Indian Buddhism, and the influence of the Gandhāra style gradually declined with the revival of a truly spiritual, traditional Indian art in the Kushan (A.D. 50-320) and Gupta (A.D. 320-647) periods. At about the same time that the Gandhāra school was at its height under the patronage of the Kushan rulers, in the early centuries of the Christian era, an entirely different style, derived from the ancient schools of Indian art, distinguished the Buddhist sculpture produced at Mathurā (modern Muttra), the southern capital of the Kushan emperors and a great artistic centre on the Jumna River, south-east of Delhi. The Mathurā images of the second and third centuries were carved from red sandstone quarried

112 BODHISATTVA MAITREYA
*Gandhāra, 2nd century*
*Dark gray schist   H. 34 3/4 in. (88.25 cm.)   939.18.1*

The Bodhisattva wears *dhoti* and shawl, two armbands, bracelets, two necklaces and amulet carrier that passes over left shoulder and under right arm. Jewelled *ushnisha* band, diadem and earrings provide additional ornaments. Lunar crescent in hair identifies the figure as Maitreya, the Buddha of the Future.

CF. H. Ingolt, *Gandhāran Art in Pakistan*, Pantheon Books, New York, 1957, p. 135, No. 289.

PUBL.: Benjamin Rowland, Jr., 'Bodhisattvas or Deified Kings: A Note on Gandhāran Sculpture', *Archives*, Vol. XV, 1961, p. 7, Fig. 1.

at Sikri, near the capital. The stone, which often has blemishes and is marked by yellow and white veins, was in its original state probably covered with polychromy and gilt to hide the imperfections of the material.

The Buddhist sculpture produced in the Mathurā workshops displays powerful spiritual qualities, combined with idealized proportions and a physical sensuousness in sharp contrast to the humanistic approach of Gandhāra sculpture. The Mathurā artists adapted some of the stylistic elements of Gandhāra art, which had ushered in the first representations of the Buddha in anthropomorphic form, yet produced purely Indian images in which the Buddha is shown as a transcendental, superhuman being, in an essentially Indian style of sculpture. The decoration on the fragment from a stupa railing (Pl. 115), with the bust of a Yakshī on the face and lotus medallions on the reverse, similarly derives from very ancient motifs of Indian art. Both the Yakshī and the lotus figure prominently in the decoration of the railings and gateways of the Bhārut and Sānchi stupas. They are thoroughly Indian in concept and meaning, and represent a definite link with India's past traditions.

Almost contemporary with the Mathurā school, another major school of Buddhist art was flourishing in east-central India, at Amarāvatī near the mouth of the Kistna River, and at Nagarjunakonda, further upstream, under the patronage of the Later Āndhra rulers (c. A.D. 50-320). The principal and most famous monument of the Later Āndhras was the Great Stupa at Amarāvatī, begun as early as c. 200 B.C. but enlarged and completed in the second century and the first half of the third century A.D. The many ruins found in the area of the Kistna River suggest, however, that countless stupas and monasteries were at one time raised here by the Āndhras. Parts of the railings and also the drum of the Amarāvatī stupa were originally covered with elaborate carvings of Buddhist subjects in the greenish-white limestone characteristic of the region. The huge casing slabs which originally covered the drum show us the appearance of the original monument and the changes made in the iconographic requirements of the stupa, compared to its simpler prototypes at Bhārut and Sānchi. The medallions and other reliefs recovered from the ruins at Amarāvatī also reveal an elegant, highly sophisticated and crowded style of sculpture. The human figures tend to be shown with elongated bodies and in complicated poses, surrounded by deep shadows and strong contrasts of light and

dark to heighten the action, and there is sometimes intense dramatic content in the scenes depicted. Simple images of the Buddha have also been recovered from this region, and usually reveal a distinct style of their own, often combining elements of both the Gandhāra and Mathurā schools. The museum, at present, has no examples to illustrate the sculptural style of the Amarāvatī region, which had a great impact not only upon the early Buddhist art of Ceylon but also upon the later art of the Pallavas, as illustrated by the great relief carving of the Descent of the Ganges at Māmallapuram, on the south-east coast, dating from the early seventh century.

The Gandhāra and Mathurā schools and the regional characteristics of Kushan sculpture were ultimately brought into harmony in the Gupta period (A.D. 320-647), a politically powerful age which produced a rich and sophisticated civilization, corresponding to that of T'ang China and Tempyō Japan. Much of India was again unified. All of northern India fell under the sway of the Gupta sovereigns, whose centre of power was once again in Magadha, in the Bengal Valley, which centuries earlier had been the seat of empire of the Mauryas. The Gandhāra region, although briefly part of the Gupta empire, was soon overrun by the White Huns and thus remained separate from India proper, and Gupta power never penetrated the south of India, where local dynasties like the Pallavas and Chalukyas succeeded the Āndhras.

The Gupta period, often considered the Classical Age of Indian art, saw the final and supreme florescence of Indian Buddhist sculpture and painting developing from the indigenous Mathurā style of the second and third centuries, which already had absorbed and adapted the influence of the Gandhāra school. The Gupta images, notably those of the two major schools of sculpture flourishing at Mathurā and at Sārnāth, show the emergence of a serene, idealized Buddha type, majestic, sophisticated and deeply moving in its spirituality. The Gupta Buddhas have lost the Graeco-Roman aspects of the Gandhāra type, but instead show a careful adherence to Indian ideals, requiring the strict observation of rigid canons of proportion and the sacred marks which distinguish the body of the Buddha. The Buddha is no longer shown as an ordinary mortal, as in the art of Gandhāra, but as an idealized, super-human being. The various Buddha types, including the standing image and the Buddha seated cross-legged in Yoga pose, the Bodhisattvas and lesser Buddhist deities all became standardized in the Gupta period and were to serve as prototypes for the Buddhist art of all of Asia. Sensuous and often gently swaying physical types, wearing thin, transparent garments which reveal beautiful yet highly abstract bodies, are the accepted Gupta formula. Such types are encountered in sculpture as well as painting, and the Gupta period achieved its perhaps most supreme and most perfect form of expression in the magnificent wall paintings at Ajanta. So firmly established and effective did the Gupta norm become that it was to exert a profound influence everywhere, from Ceylon and Java to Cambodia and Siam, and ultimately upon the entire Far East.

The fortunes of the Gupta period declined following the invasion of the White Huns and their conquest of Gandhāra early in the sixth century. For a while, the glories of the Gupta empire were revived by Harsha of Kanauj (A.D. 606-647), but the Gupta florescence of the arts had passed its peak in the fifth century and, by the seventh century, Buddhism had largely disappeared in northern India. Hinduism, which had never been completely extinguished, once more rose to a position of prominence and, in the centuries which were to follow, Hinduism rather than the religion of Śākyamuni was responsible for the continuing greatness of Indian art in sculpture, painting and notably architecture. Buddhism continued to linger in isolated areas and its final phase of development took place in the Bengal Valley, under the patronage of the Pāla and Sena Dynasties (A.D. 730-1197). From the seventh century on, Bodh Gayā and Nalanda, the latter famous as a university city and for the number of its monastic establishments, were the principal centres of Buddhism and, according to the reports of Hsüan-tsang, the famous pilgrim from T'ang China, the Mahāyāna form of Buddhism was then flourishing.

The Gupta period had made its mark. The norm established for the iconography and style of Buddhist sculpture and painting had a lasting influence upon the later Buddhist art of Asia. The Gupta style was perpetuated in India, with only slight modifications, in the workshops of the Pāla period; and the collection has a splendid example in the form of a Stele, with standing Buddha and attendants (Pl. 116). The image, carved in the black chlorite stone characteristic of the Pāla workshops, dates from the ninth century. It essentially continues the tradition of the Sārnāth school in the Buddha's smooth, sheath-like garment of which only the borders are visible, though the representation is drier and more stereotyped than in the Gupta examples. In the slightly later, eleventh century stele with a representation of Sūrya, the Aryan solar deity (Pl. 117), the smooth surface treatment and the flawless proportions of the principal figure still evidence Gupta influence, although in modified form. However, the iconography of the image also reflects the increasing impact of Hinduism upon the art of Bengal and Bihar in the eleventh and twelfth centuries.

The revival of Hinduism which followed the collapse of the Gupta empire gave rise to the great Medieval period, an era famous for its magnificent temples and rich outpouring of sculpture. Sculpture was based upon the vast Hindu pantheon and the legends of the Hindu epics, the *Rāmāyana* and the *Mahābhārata*, and was intended primarily as a decorative overlay for the soaring spires and massive sanctuaries of the enormous temples. The huge, towering structures raised at Khajurāho in central India, at Bhuvaneśvar in Orissa, and under the Cholas and their successors at Tanjore and other cities in the south, bear witness to the tremendous enterprise, skill and vision of the builders of the temples, and of the sculptors who decorated them. In the south of India, under the Pallava (*c*. A.D. 500-750) and Chola (*c*. A.D. 850-1310) rulers, the art of casting images in bronze was also perfected to a high degree. The splendid Natarāja, representing the Dance of Śiva, illustrates one of the most popular and most characteristic forms of these images (Pl. 122).

The powerful Chola image of Maheśvarī or Kālī (Pl. 118) and the elegant Female Torso (Pl. 119) from north-central India, are excellent examples of Hindu sculpture from the Medieval era. The former, emotionally powerful and ferocious, and the latter, sensuous and provocative, admirably express the strength and vitality of Hindu sculpture. The bronze Yakshī (Pl. 120), a work of the Chalukya period from the eighth or ninth century, derives essentially from the tree and fertility spirits of the early Buddhist age, and thus bears witness to the basic unity and traditional character of Indian art.

113  STAIR-RISER RELIEFS
*Gandhāra, 2nd century*
*Soapstone  924.27.1   H. 7 1/8 in. (18.1 cm.); l. 20 3/8 in. (51.7 cm.)*
*930.192   H. 6 1/4 in. (15.8 cm.); l. 16 7/8 in. (42.8 cm.)*

Left, relief of classical type with male and female donors dressed in princely costume, consisting of Indian *dhoti* and shawl. Four of the figures holding flowers; two in centre standing empty-handed. Indo-Corinthian half-column, set in rectangular niche, frames scene on each side.

Right, relief of similar style, with one female and five male figures, but wearing classical garments and carrying musical instruments. Woman wears chiton and himation and holds tall wine goblet.

The reliefs are stylistically related to a number of similar reliefs from the Gandhāra region. Typical of these reliefs is the treatment of the drapery in terms of closely spread, parallel lines and zigzag folds of classical type. There is no overlapping, each figure standing isolated against a plain background. Frontal poses have been carefully avoided.

CF. H. Ingholt, *Gandhāran Art in Pakistan*, New York, 1957, Pl. IV, and Nos. 411-414; text, pp. 26, 161.

**114** RELIEF

*Gandhāra, 2nd – 3rd century*

*Dark gray schist  H. 9 5/8 in. (23.6 cm.); l. 20 in, (50.8 cm.)  Purchased with funds from the Reuben Wells Leonard Bequest  939.17.19*

Slightly convex panel. The unusual decoration shows a group of male figures, bearded and with long hair, wearing Iranian type costumes and carrying swords attached in Iranian fashion. The garments consist of long trousers and heavy, three-quarter length tunics, tied by a belt, and with flaring folds over the thighs. The figures are shown in a variety of relaxed poses and views, recalling the sarcophagi from the southeast necropolis at Palmyra, and are arranged in pairs engaged in animated conversation. On one side

is a niche with yakshinī standing on a bulbous waterpot and grasping the frond of a stylized palm tree. The yakshinī, who is nude to the waist, except for a necklace, wears a *dhoti*. She is standing on her right foot; the left leg is bent at the knee, with only the toes touching the ground. The combination of Western Asiatic male figures and Indian yakshinī used as a decorative motif reflects the hybrid aspects of Gandhāra art.

CF. H. Ingholt, *Gandhāran Art in Pakistan*, New York, 1957, No. 419. (Worshippers in Iranian costume.)

PUBL.: *Palmyrene and Gandhāran Sculpture*, Yale University Art Gallery, 1954, No. 24; J. Rosenfield, *Dynastic Arts of the Kūshan*, Harvard, 1967, frontispiece and Fig. 59.

115 FRAGMENT OF STUPA RAILING PILLAR
*From Mathurā   Kushan period, 1st – 2nd century*
*Red sandstone   H. 13 1/2 in. (34.3 cm.); w. 7 5/16 in. (18.6 cm.)*
*959.119*

Yakshī or tree spirit holding mirror in her left hand. Two lotus
medallions in relief on reverse. Oblong holes on right side of pillar
to hold horizontal cross bars of stupa railing.
The yakshī is the female counterpart of the yaksha. They are nature
spirits representing the fertility of the soil, the flowing sap of trees,
and, in a larger sense, symbolize the origin of all life. The yakshīs
were worshipped since earliest times in India but were later adopted
by Buddhism. Together with the yakshas they are commonly found
as decorative motifs on the railings and gates of ancient stupas.

116 STELE
*Pāla period, 9th century*
*Black chlorite stone   H. 25 5/16 in. (64.3 cm.)   961.171*

The image is typical of the style which distinguished Buddhist
sculpture in its last phase of development, following the breakup of
the Gupta empire. Under the Pāla and Sena rulers, Buddhist art
flourished in eastern India, in Bihar and Bengal, from the eighth
through the twelfth century. The stele shows a Buddha standing on
a double lotus accompanied by two Lokeśvara, one of them carrying
a *chattra* (umbrella). The other attendant holds a vase and fly-whisk.
The small kneeling figure on the left with hands in an attitude of
prayer probably represents a donor. There are two pagodas in relief
at the level of the Buddha's head. The central figure, with snail-
shell curls and smooth, transparent drapery which reveals the body
underneath, essentially follows the Gupta tradition of the Sārnāth
school.

PUBL.: T. A. Heinrich, *Art Treasures in the Royal Ontario Museum*,
Toronto, 1963, p. 83.

**117** STELE

*Bihar or Bengal    Pāla period, 11th century*
*Black chlorite stone    H. 34 in. (86.3 cm.)    964.11*

Sūrya, in the centre, is riding the solar chariot, pulled by seven horses and driven by Aruna, the Sun god's legless charioteer, appearing above the central horse in the foremost plane of the relief. To the left and right are two female archers, Ușā and Pratyūsā, personifying the different aspects of dawn driving away darkness. In front of the Sun god is the small figure of his wife, Ușas, the Dawn of the World. His other two wives, each holding a fly-whisk in the right hand, flank him on either side. Beside them stands Piṇgala, the recorder of the Sun god, heavy-limbed and bearded, carrying ink pot and pen, and on Sūrya's left, the youthful Daṇda, the Sun god's measurer.

Sūrya has his hands raised to the chest and holds a lotus flower in each hand at the level of his face. He wears tight-fitting trousers, high boots and seems naked to the waist, except for thin scarves crossed in front. He is adorned with elaborate jewelry, including earrings, necklace and torque, sacred thread (*yajñopavita*), amulets, bracelets and jewelled belt. A sword is attached to his left side.

On the high back of the stele, on the left and right, is a leogryph (*śārdūlā*) towering over an elephant on a lotus flower  The elephant is the support of the world and serves as a symbol of the earth. The leogryph symbolizes the solar power of manifestation. Above the leogryph and elephant groups appear vinaras, playing musical instruments, and flying male divinities on clouds, carrying garlands and supporting their music-playing wives on their legs. At the centre of the pointed top is a large 'face of glory' flanked by foliate scrolls.

A Pāla stele of similar iconographic content in the Philadelphia Museum of Art is described by Stella Kramrisch, *Indian Sculpture in the Philadelphia Museum of Art*, Philadelphia, 1960, No. 63, Pls. 24-25.

118  MĀHEŚVARĪ or KĀLĪ
*South India, Chola Dynasty, 10th – 11th century*
*Stone   H. 43 11/16 in. (111 cm.)   956.181*

Seated female figure, four-armed and holding battle-axe, tongs and
bowl. Massive hair with skull and twined snakes in crown. Deity
wears torque and necklaces, bracelets, snake armlets and sacred
thread passing between breasts.
The figure symbolizes one of Śiva's fierce aspects. It represents one of
the Sapta Mātrikas (Seven Mothers), each of which is a *śakti*
representing an aspect of Śiva's energies.

CF. *Handbook*, Nelson Gallery of Art – Atkins Museum, Kansas City,
1959, p. 228.

PUBL.: *The Sculpture of Greater India*, C. T. Loo and Co., New York,
1942, No. 33; T. A. Heinrich, *Art Treasures in the Royal Ontario
Museum*, Toronto, 1963, pp. 84-85.

OPPOSITE

119 FEMALE TORSO
*North-central India, 11th century*
*Reddish brown sandstone   H. 19 1/4 in. (49.5 cm.)   934.31.7*

The triple bend and axial distortion as well as voluptuous quality
of the torso are characteristic of Hindu sculpture of this period. These
elements were ultimately inspired by the ancient Indian yakshī or
tree spirit, as represented more than a thousand years earlier on the
gateways of the Great Stupa at Sāñchi.
The exterior walls of the temples raised during the Hindu renaissance, which followed the breakup of the Gupta empire and decline
of Buddhism in the seventh century, were adorned with a rich overlay of sculptured decoration. The arts of architecture and sculpture
thus became thoroughly interwoven in this period. The great temples
at Khajurāho, in central India, raised by the Chandela Rājput
sovereigns between 950 and 1050 A.D. are a striking example of the
new trend in Indian architecture. The effectiveness of these shrines,
like that of countless other Hindu temples, derives from a combination and perfect balance of elegant proportions, sweeping contours
and dynamic ornamentation. The decorative scheme of the Hindu
temple usually centred around the depiction of celestial beauties
and their escorts, various sacred figures, plants, animals and birds.
The Museum's figure once formed part of such a decorative ensemble.

PUBL.: *An Illustrated Catalogue of Objects of Art*, Edward Goldston,
Ltd., London, n.d., p. 14 (left); T. A. Heinrich, *Art Treasures in the
Royal Ontario Museum*, 1963, p. 86-87.

120 YAKSHĪ
*Deccan, Chalukya period, 8th – 9th century*
*Bronze   H. 9 in. (22.9 cm.)   939.17.20*

Standing in *tribhanga* ('three-bend') pose, with weight on left foot
and left hip thrown out. Nude except for thin *dhoti* and jewelry.
The type derives from the ancient Indian yakshī, a tree or fertility
spirit worshipped in India since ancient times. The right hand
holds the stem of a lotus.

PUBL.: *Bronzes of India and Greater India*, Rhode Island School of
Design, 1955, p. 13, No. 52; *Master Bronzes of India*, The Art Institute of Chicago, 1965, No. 20.

**121 STANDING BUDDHA**

*From Negapatam, Tanjore District, Madras   South India, 13th century*
*Bronze   H. 15 7/8 in. (40.3 cm.)   957.152.2*

Right hand raised in *abhaya mudrā* ('do not fear'), left extended with palm turned upward. Buddha standing on lotus base, mounted on rectangular plinth. The *dhoti* and thin, diaphanous mantle with parallel folds across the front of the body correspond to the Gupta style of the Mathurā school. The head is surmounted by a flame *ushnisha*. The snail-shell curls of hair, characteristic of the Gupta Buddhas, are reduced to small bosses.

For stylistic features of the Buddha, CF. *The Art of India and Pakistan. A Commemorative Catalogue of the Exhibition held at the Royal Academy of Arts, London, 1947-48*, Pl. 60, No. 331.

OPPOSITE

**122 NATARĀJA**

*South India, Madras Province, 13th – 14th century*
*Bronze   H. 40 in. (101.6 cm.); w. 34 1/2 in. (87.6 cm.)   938.44*

This image of Śiva as Natarāja (Lord of the Dance) symbolizes the Cosmic Activity, the eternal process of creation, preservation, destruction, incarnation and release or salvation. Śiva, who is four-armed, holds the drum of creation in the upper right hand, the flame of destruction in the upper left. The lower right is in *abhaya mudrā* ('do not fear'), the outstretched left hand points at the raised foot, the refuge of the soul, while the right foot tramples upon the dwarf-demon, Apasmāra-purusha, crushed to the ground and lying on his right side. The hair is dressed high and crowned with peacock feathers, bearing a crescent moon and cobra. The lower locks, cast in thin strands and supporting the small figure of Gaṅgā (the Ganges fallen from heaven and lost in Śiva's hair), end in curls and are whirling with the movement of the dance. The flaming circle (*tiruvāsi*), within which Śiva performs the dance, symbolizes the Universe. The icon is supported on a double lotus base, with holes in the sides for the insertion of poles to carry the image in processions at times of festivals.

CF. A. K. Coomaraswamy, *Catalogue of the Indian Collections in the Museum of Fine Arts, Boston*, Boston, 1923, Pts. 1-2, Pl. XLV, No. 21. 1828; H. Zimmer, *The Art of Indian Asia*, New York, 1955, Vol. II, Pls. 411-414; Museum van Aziatische Kunst in het Rijiksmuseum, Amsterdam, *Catalogue*, n.d., No. 209.

PUBL.: F. St. G. Spendlove, 'The Royal Ontario Museum's Dancing Śiva,' *Gazette des Beaux Arts*, Vol. XXV, Jan., 1944, pp. 50-60; 'A Bronze Figure of Śiva as Natarāja (Lord of the Dance),' *R.O.M.A. Bulletin*, No. 16, April, 1949, pp. 2-5.

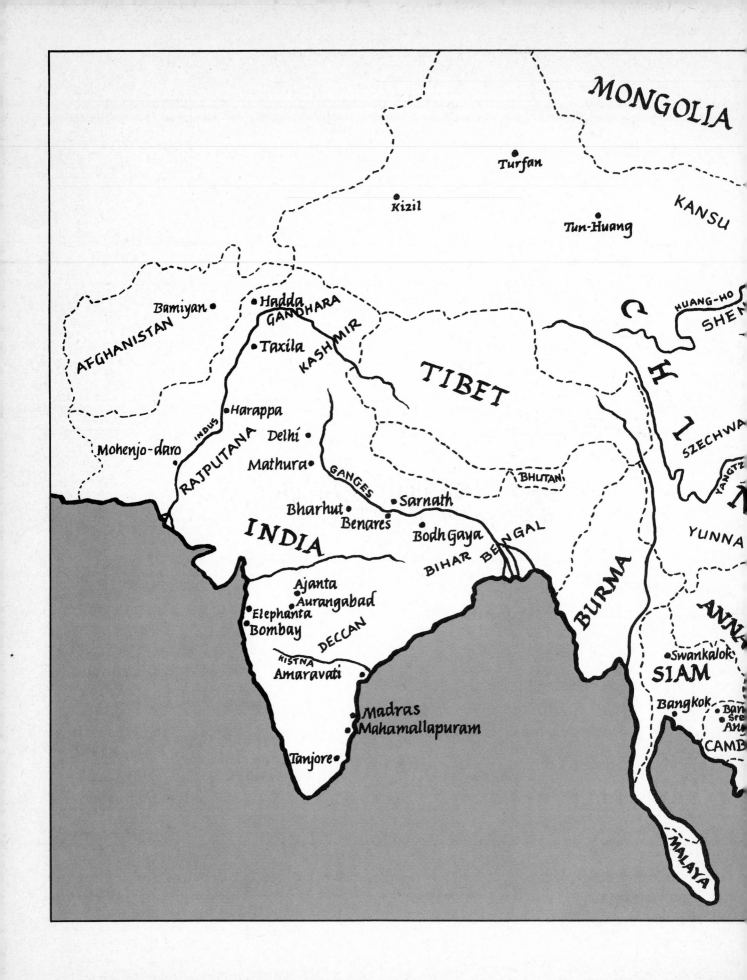

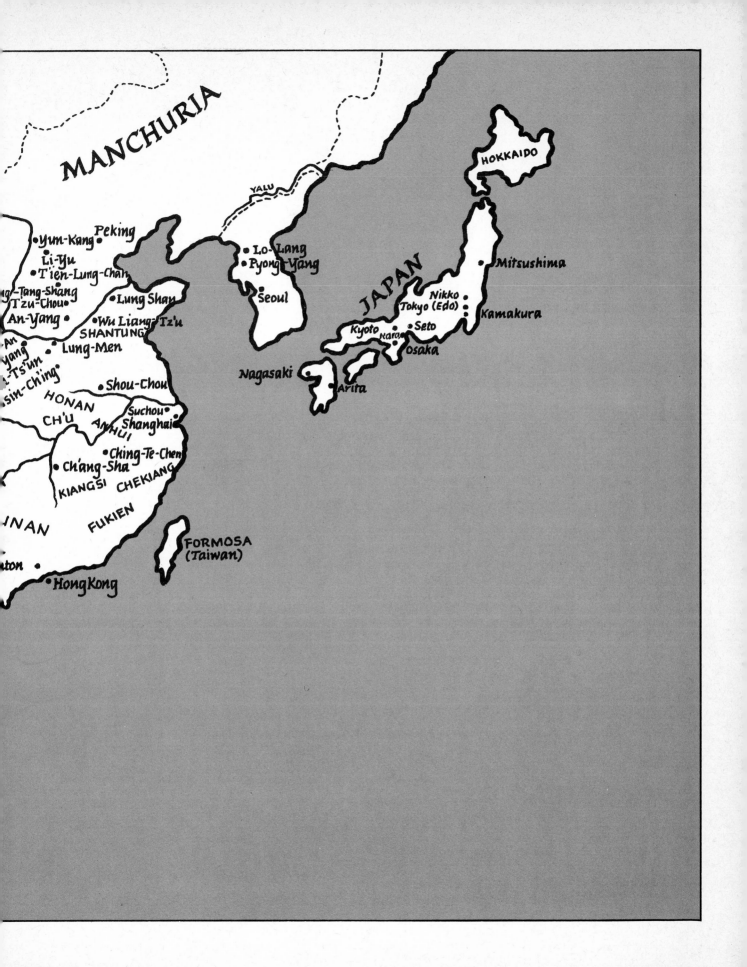

# Chronology

## INDIAN ART

Pre-Buddhist Period (– c. 322 B.C.)
   *Indus Valley Period (c. 2300 – 1700 B.C.)*
   *Vedic Period (1500 – 800 B.C.)*
   *Śaiśunaga-Nanda Period (643 – 322 B.C.)*
Period of Buddhist Ascendancy
   *Maurya Period (322 – 185 B.C.)*
   *Śunga Period (185 – 72 B.C.)*
   *Early Āndhra Period (72 B.C. – c. A.D. 50)*
   *Kushan Period (including Gandhāra) (c. A.D. 50 – 320)*
   *Later Āndhra Period (c. A.D. 50 – 320)*
   *Gupta Period (including Harsha) (c. A.D. 320 – 647)*
Medieval Period (c. A.D. 600 – c. 1200)
   *Pāla and Sena Periods (Bengal) (A.D. 730 – 1197)*
   *Pāllava Period (South) (c. A.D. 500 – c. 750)*
   *First Chalukyan Period (North) (A.D. 550 – 753)*
   *Rāshtrakūtan Period (A.D. 753 – c. 900)*
   *Medieval Kingdoms of Rājputāna and the Deccan (North)*
      *(c. A.D. 900 – c. 1190)*
   *Chola Period (South) (Mid-9th Century A.D. – 1310)*
Later Medieval Period (A.D. 1200 – 1756)
   *Sultanate of Delhi (North) (c. A.D. 1200 – 14th Century)*
   *Vijayanagar Period (South) (A.D. 1336 – 1646)*
   *Madura Period (South) (A.D. 1646 – c. 1900)*
   *Mughal Dynasty (A.D. 1526 – 1756)*
   *Rajput Style (North) (c. A.D. 1500 – c. 1900)*

## KOREAN ART

Naknang (Han Chinese Dominance) (108 B.C. – A.D. 313)
Three Kingdoms (57 B.C. – A.D. 668)
   *Kokuryo Dynasty (37 B.C. – A.D. 668)*
   *Paekche Dynasty (18 B.C. – A.D. 663)*
   *Old Silla Dynasty (57 B.C. – A.D. 668)*
Unified Silla Kingdom (A.D. 668 – 935)
Koryu Period (A.D. 918 – 1392)
Yi (Li) Dynasty (A.D. 1392 – 1910)

## CHINESE ART

Shang Dynasty (1523 – 1028 B.C.)
   *Latter half (Capital at An-yang) (1300 – 1028 B.C.)*
Chou Dynasty (1027 – 256 B.C.)
   *Western Chou Dynasty (1027 – 771 B.C.)*
   *Eastern Chou Dynasty (771 – 256 B.C.)*
   *Period of the Spring and Autumn Annals*
      *(722 – 481 B.C.)*
   *Period of the Warring States (481 – 221 B.C.)*

THE CHOU PERIOD MAY ALSO BE DIVIDED STYLISTICALLY:
   *Early Chou Period (1027 – c. 900 B.C.)*
   *Middle Chou Period (c. 900 – 600 B.C.)*
   *Late Chou Period (c. 600 – 222 B.C.)*

Ch'in Dynasty (221 – 206 B.C.)
Han Dynasty (206 B.C. – A.D. 220)
   *Western Han Dynasty* (206 B.C. – A.D. 9)
   *Eastern Han Dynasty* (A.D. 25 – 220)
Three Kingdoms (A.D. 220 – 280)
   *Wei Kingdom* (A.D. 220 – 280)
   *Shu Kingdom* (A.D. 221 – 263)
   *Wei Kingdom* (A.D. 220 – 265)
Western Chin Dynasty (A.D. 265 – 316)
Six Dynasties (A.D. 220 – 589)
   *Northern Dynasties* (A.D. 317 – 589)
     *Northern Wei Dynasty* (A.D. 386 – 535)
     *Northern Ch'i Dynasty* (A.D. 550 – 577)
     *Northern Chou Dynasty* (A.D. 557 – 581)
   *Southern Dynasties* (A.D. 420 – 589)
Sui Dynasty (A.D. 581 – 618)
T'ang Dynasty (A.D. 618 – 906)
Five Dynasties (A.D. 907 – 960)
   *Liao Kingdom (in Manchuria)* (A.D. 916 – 1124)
Sung Dynasty (A.D. 960 – 1279)
   *Northern Sung Dynasty* (A.D. 960 – 1127)
   *Southern Sung Dynasty* (A.D. 1127 – 1279)
Yüan Dynasty (A.D. 1280 – 1368)
Ming Dynasty (A.D. 1368 – 1644)
  REIGNS:
   *Yung Lo* (A.D. 1403 – 1424)
   *Hsüan-tê* (A.D. 1426 – 1435)
   *Ch'êng-hua* (A.D. 1465 – 1487)
   *Chêng-tê* (A.D. 1506 – 1521)
   *Chia-ching* (A.D. 1522 – 1566)
   *Wan-li* (A.D. 1573 – 1619)

Ch'ing Dynasty (A.D. 1644 – 1912)
  REIGNS:
   *K'ang-hsi* (A.D. 1662 – 1722)
   *Yung-chêng* (A.D. 1723 – 1735)
   *Ch'ien-lung* (A.D. 1736 – 1795)
   *Chia-ch'ing* (A.D. 1796 – 1820)
Republic (1912 –    )

## JAPANESE ART

Pre-Buddhist Age (Prior to the mid-sixth century A.D.)
Asuka Period (Suikō) (A.D. 538 – 645)
Nara Period (A.D. 645 – 794)
   *Early Nara Period (Hakuhō)* (A.D. 645 – 710)
   *Late Nara Period (Tempyō)* (A.D. 710 – 794)
Heian Period (A.D. 794 – 1185)
   *Early Heian Period (Jōgan)* (A.D. 794 – 897)
   *Late Heian Period (Fujiwara)* (A.D. 897 – 1185)
Kamakura Period (A.D. 1185 – 1334)
Nambokucho Period (A.D. 1334 – 1392)
Muromachi Period (Ashikaga) (A.D. 1334 – 1573)
Momoyama Period (A.D. 1573 – 1615)
Edo Period (Tokugawa) (A.D. 1615 – 1868)
   *Early Edo Period* (A.D. 1615 – 1716)
   *Late Edo Period* (A.D. 1716 – 1868)
Modern Japan (A.D. 1868 – to date)

AKIYAMA, Terukazu. *Japanese Painting*, Lausanne, 1961

Arts Council of Great Britain. *Chinese Blue and White Porcelain, 14th to 19th Centuries; an Exhibition Organized by the Arts Council of Great Britain and The Oriental Ceramic Society, December 16th, 1953 to January 23rd, 1954 at the Arts Council Gallery*, London, 1953

Arts Council of Great Britain. *The Arts of the Ch'ing Dynasty; an Exhibition Organized by the Arts Council of Great Britain and The Oriental Ceramic Society, May 26th to July 2nd, 1964 at the Arts Council Gallery*, London, 1965

Arts Council of Great Britain. *The Arts of the Ming Dynasty; an Exhibition Organized by the Arts Council of Great Britain and The Oriental Ceramic Society, November 15th to December 14th, 1957 at the Arts Council Gallery*, London, 1958

Arts Council of Great Britain. *The Arts of the Sung Dynasty; an Exhibition Organized by the Arts Council of Great Britain and The Oriental Ceramic Society, June 16th to July 23rd, 1960 at the Arts Council Gallery*, London, 1960

Arts Council of Great Britain. *The Arts of the T'ang Dynasty; an Exhibition Organized by the Arts Council of Great Britain and The Oriental Ceramic Society, February 25th to March 30th, 1955 at the Arts Council Gallery*, London, 1955

ASHTON, Sir Leigh (ed.). *The Art of India and Pakistan* (Catalogue of the Exhibition of the Royal Academy of Arts, London, 1947-48) London, 1950

AYERS, John. *The Seligman Collection of Oriental Art: Vol II, Chinese and Korean Pottery and Porcelain*, London, 1964

BACHHOFER, Ludwig. *A Short History of Chinese Art*, New York, 1946

BARNARD, Noel. *Bronze Casting and Bronze Alloys in Ancient China*, Canberra, Australia and Nagoya, 1961

BUHOT, Jean. *Histoire des Arts du Japan*, Paris, 1949

CAHILL, James. *Chinese Painting*, New York, 1960

CHANG, Kwang-chih. *The Archaeology of Ancient China*, New Haven and London, 1963

CHENG, Te-k'un. *Archaeology in China: Vol. I, Prehistoric China*, Cambridge, England, 1959
——— *Archaeology in China, Vol. II: Shang China*, Cambridge, England, 1960
——— *Archaeology in China, Vol. III: Chou China*, Cambridge, England, 1963

*Ch'uan-kuo chi-pên chien-shieh kung-chêng chung ch'u t'u wên wu chên-lan t'u-lu* (Exhibition of Chinese Cultural Objects Excavated at Construction Sites Since 1949), 2 vols., Peking, 1955

CONSTEN, Eleanor v. Erdberg. *Das Alte China*, Stuttgart, 1958

COOMARASWAMY, Ananda K. *A History of Indian and Indonesian Art*, New York, 1927

D'ARGENCÉ, René-Yvon Levebre. *Ancient Chinese Bronzes in the Avery Brundage Collection*, Berkeley, 1966

DAVIDSON, LeRoy. *The Lotus Sutra in Chinese Art*, New Haven, 1954

FEDDERSEN, Martin. *Chinese Decorative Art, a Handbook for Collectors and Connoisseurs*, London, 1961

FISCHER, Klaus. *Schöpfungen Indischer Kunst*, Cologne, 1959

GARNER, Sir Harry. *Chinese and Japanese Cloisonné Enamels*, London, 1962
——— *Oriental Blue and White*, London, 1954

GOMPERTZ, G. St. G. M. *Chinese Celadon Wares*, London, 1958

GOODRICH, Luther C. *A Short History of the Chinese People*, New York, 1943

GRAY, Basil. *Early Chinese Pottery and Porcelain*, London, 1953

GROUSSET, René. *La Chine et son Art* (Editions d'histoire et d'art), Paris, 1951

GYLLENSVÄRD, Bo. 'T'ang Gold and Silver,' *Bulletin of the Museum of Far Eastern Antiquities*, Vol. XXIX, 1957

HANSFORD, S. Howard. *Glossary of Chinese Art and Archaeology*, London, 1954
——— *The Seligman Collection of Oriental Art: Vol. I, Chinese, Central Asian and Luristan Bronzes and Chinese Jades and Sculptures*, London, 1957

HASKINS, John F. 'Recent Excavations in China,' *Archives of the Chinese Art Society of America*, Vol. X, 1956

HEUSDEN, Willem van. *Ancient Chinese Bronzes of the Shang and Chou Dynasties; an Illustrated Catalogue of the van Heusden Collection*, Tokyo, 1952

HONEY, William Bowyer. *Ceramic Art of China and Other Countries of the Far East*, London, 1945

INGHOLT, Harold, and ISLAY, Lyons. *Gandhāran Art in Pakistan*, New York, 1957

JENYNS, Soame. *Japanese Porcelain*, London, 1965
——— *Later Chinese Porcelain, The Ch'ing Dynasty*, London, 1951, 2d ed., 1959, 3rd ed., 1965
——— *Ming Pottery and Porcelain*, London, 1953

JENYNS, Soame, and WATSON, William. *Chinese Art: The Minor Arts*, New York, 1963

KARLGREN, Bernhard. *A Catalogue of the Chinese Bronzes in the Alfred F. Pillsbury Collection*, Minneapolis, 1952
——— 'Huai and Han,' *Bulletin of the Museum of Far Eastern Antiquities*, Vol. XIII, 1941
——— 'New Studies on Chinese Bronzes,' *Bulletin of the Museum of Far Eastern Antiquities*, Vol. IX, 1937
——— 'Yin and Chou in Chinese Bronzes,' *Bulletin of the Museum of Far Eastern Antiquities*, Vol. VIII, 1936

KELLY, Charles F., and CH'EN, Meng-chia. *Chinese Bronzes from the Buckingham Collection*, Art Institute of Chicago, 1946

KOYAMA, Fujio, and FIGGESS, John. *Two Thousand Years of Oriental Ceramics*, New York, 1960

KRAMRISCH, Stella. *The Art of India*, London, 1954

KUNO, Takeshi (ed.). *A Guide to Japanese Sculpture*, Mayuyama and Co., Tokyo, 1963

LEE, Jean Gordon. *Ming Blue and White*, Philadelphia Museum of Art, 1949

LEE, Sherman E. *Buddhist Art*, Detroit Institute of Arts, 1942
——— *Chinese Landscape Painting*, 2d rev. ed., Cleveland Museum of Art, 1962
——— *A History of Far Eastern Art*, New York, 1964
——— *Japanese Decorative Style*, Cleveland Museum of Art, 1961
——— 'Sung Ceramics in the Light of Recent Japanese Research,' *Artibus Asiae*, Vol. XI, 1948, No. 3, pp. 164-175

LETH, André. *Kinesisk Kunst i Kunstindustri Museet*, Copenhagen, 1959

LI, Chi. *The Beginnings of Chinese Civilization; Three Lectures Illustrated with Finds at Anyang*, Seattle, 1957

LION-GOLDSCHMIDT, Daisy. *Chinese Art: Bronze, Jade, Sculpture, Ceramics*, New York, 1960

LODGE, John E.; WENLEY, Archibald G; and POPE, John A. *A Descriptive Catalogue of Chinese Bronzes*, Smithsonian Institution, Washington, D.C., 1946

LOEHR, Max. *Chinese Bronze Age Weapons*, Ann Arbor, 1956
——— *Relics of Ancient China From the Collection of Dr. Paul Singer*, The Asia Society, Inc., New York, 1965
——— 'The Bronze Styles of the Anyang Period,' *Archives of the Chinese Art Society of America*, Vol. VII, 1954

MAHLER, Jane Gaston. *The Westerners Among the Figurines of the T'ang Dynasty of China*, Rome, 1959

MARSHALL, Sir John. *The Buddhist Art of Gandhāra*, Cambridge, England, 1960
——— *Taxila*, 3 vols., London, 1951

*Masterpieces of Korean Art. An Exhibition under the Auspices of the Government of the Republic of Korea*, National Gallery of Art, Washington, D.C., 1957

MAYUYAMA, Junkichi (ed.). *Chinese Ceramics in the West, a Compendium of Chinese Ceramic Masterpieces in European and American Collections*, Tokyo, 1960

McCUNE, Evelyn. *The Arts of Korea*, Rutland, Vermont and Tokyo, 1962

MEDLEY, Margaret. *Illustrated Catalogue of Ming Polychrome Wares in the Percival David Foundation of Chinese Art*, London, 1966
——— *Porcelains Decorated in Underglaze Blue and Copper Red in the Percival David Foundation of Chinese Art*, London, 1963

MINAMOTO, Hoshu, and HENDERSON, Harold G. *An Illustrated History of Japanese Art*, Kyoto, 1939

MIZUNO, Seiichi. *Bronze and Stone Sculpture of China from the Yin to the T'ang Dynasty*, partially trans. Yuichi Kajiyama and Burton Watson, Tokyo, 1960
——*Bronzes and Jades of Ancient China*, trans. J. O. Gauntlett, Tokyo, 1959
——— *Chinese Stone Sculpture*, Tokyo, 1950

*Mostra d'art Cinese* (Exhibition of Chinese Art at the Doges' Palace), Venice, 1954

MUNICH, Haus der Kunst. *1000 Jahre Chinesische Malerei*, Munich, 1959

Oakland Art Museum. *Japanese Ceramics from Ancient to Modern Times, Selected from Collections in Japan and America* (February 4 through 26, 1961), ed. Fujio Koyama, Oakland, California, 1961

PAINE, Robert T., and SOPER, Alexander C. *The Art and Architecture of Japan*, Baltimore, 1955, 2d ed., 1960

PALMGREN, Nils. *Selected Chinese Antiquities from the Collection of Gustaf Adolph, Crown Prince of Sweden*, Stockholm, 1948

Peking Palace Museum. *Ts'ang tz'u hsüan-chi* (The Selected Porcelains from the Collection of the Palace Museum), 2 vols., Peking, 1962

POPE, John Alexander. *Chinese Porcelains from the Ardebil Shrine*, Washington, D.C., 1956
——— *Fourteenth-Century Blue and White. A Group of Chinese Porcelains in the Topkapu Sarayi Müzesi, Istanbul*, Washington, 1952

ROSENFIELD, J. *Dynastic Arts of the Kushan*, Harvard, 1967

ROWLAND, Benjamin Jr. *The Art and Architecture of India*, Baltimore, 1953
——— *The Evolution of the Buddha Image*, The Asia Society, Inc., New York, 1963
——— *The Harvard Outline and Reading Lists for Oriental Art*, Cambridge, Mass., 1952

RUDOLPH, Richard. *Han Tomb Art of West China*, Berkeley and Los Angeles, 1951

SAKANISHI, Shio. *The Spirit of the Brush*, London, 1939

SALMONY, Alfred. *Carved Jade of Ancient China*, Berkeley, 1938

SANSOM, George Bailey. *Japan, A Short Cultural History*, New York, 1931

*Sekai toji zenshu* (Catalogue of World's Ceramics), 16 vols., Tokyo, 1955-56

SICKMAN, Laurence, and SOPER, Alexander C. *The Art and Architecture of China*, Baltimore, 1956, 2d ed., 1960

SIRÉN, Osvald. *The Chinese on the Art of Painting*, Peking, 1936
——— *Chinese Painting: Leading Masters and Principles*, 7 vols., New York, 1956-58
——— *Chinese Sculpture: From the Fifth to the Fourteenth Century*, 4 vols., London, 1925

Society of Friends of Eastern Art. *Index of Japanese Painters*, Tokyo, 1959

SULLIVAN, Michael. *The Birth of Landscape Painting in China*, London, 1962
——— *Chinese Ceramics, Bronzes and Jades in the Collection of Sir Alan and Lady Barlow*, London, 1963
——— *An Introduction to Chinese Art*, London, 1961

SUMITOMO, Baron Kichizaemon. *Sen-oku sei-shō* (Catalogue of the Collection of Chinese Bronzes Owned by Baron Sumitomo), 2 vols., Osaka, 1912

SWANN, Peter C. *Art of China, Korea and Japan*, New York, 1963
——— *Chinese Painting*, Paris, 1958
——— *An Introduction to the Arts of Japan*, Oxford, 1958

Taichung National Palace Museum. *Three Hundred Masterpieces of Chinese Painting in the Palace Museum*, 6 vols., Tokyo, 1959

*Toki zenshu* (Ceramic Series: Collective Catalogue of Pottery and Porcelain of Different Periods in Japan, China and Korea), 28 vols., Tokyo, 1957

Tokyo National Museum. *Chinese Arts of the Sung and Yüan Periods*, Tokyo, 1961
——— *Pageant of Japanese Art*, 6 vols., Tokyo, 1952

TRUBNER, Henry. *Arts of the Han Dynasty*, Chinese Art Society of America, New York, 1961
——— *The Arts of the T'ang Dynasty*, Los Angeles County Museum, January 8th to February 17th, 1957
——— *Chinese Ceramics*, Los Angeles County Museum, March 14th to April 27th, 1952

UMEHARA, Sueji. *Nihon shucho shina kodo seikwa* (Selected Relics of Ancient Chinese Bronzes from Collections in Japan), Osaka, 1959
——— *Rakuyo kinson kobo shuei* (Catalogue of Selected Relics from the Ancient Tombs of Chin-ts'un, Loyang), Kyoto, 1937
——— *Sen-oku sei-shō* (The Collection of Old Bronzes of Baron Sumitomo), Kyoto, 1934
——— *Shina-kodo seikwa* (Selected Relics of Ancient Chinese Bronzes from Collections in Europe and America), 5 vols., Osaka, 1933

WARNER, Langdon. *The Enduring Art of Japan*, Cambridge, Mass., 1952

WATSON, William. *Ancient Chinese Bronzes*, London, 1962
——— *Archaeology in China*, London, 1960
——— *China Before the Han Dynasty*, Vol. XXIII of *Ancient Peoples and Places*, ed. Dr. Glyn Daniel, London, c. 1960

WHITE, William C. *Bronze Culture of Ancient China. An Archaeological Study of Bronze Objects from Northern Honan, Dating from about 1400 B.C. – 771 B.C.*, Toronto, 1956
——— *Chinese Temple Frescoes*, Toronto, 1940
——— *Tombs of Old Lo-yang*, Shanghai, 1934
——— *Tomb Tile Pictures of Ancient China*, Toronto, 1939

WILLETTS, William. *Chinese Art*, 2 vols., London, 1958
——— *Foundations of Chinese Art*, London, 1965

YAMADA, Chisaburoh F. (ed.). *Decorative Arts of Japan*, Tokyo, 1964

YASHIRO, Yukio (ed.). *Art Treasures of Japan*, 2 vols., Tokyo, 1960

YETTS, W. Percival. *The Cull Chinese Bronzes*, London, 1939

ZIMMER, Heinrich. *The Art of Indian Asia*, 2 vols., New York, 1955

PERIODICALS

*Archives of the Chinese Art Society of America*, New York
*Artibus Asiae*, Ascona
*The Bulletin of the Museum of Far Eastern Antiquities*, Stockholm
*K'ao Ku* (Chinese Archaeological Reports), Peking
*K'ao-ku hsüeh-pao* (The Chinese Journal of Archaeology), Peking
*The Kokka*, Tokyo
*Lalit Kala* (A Journal of Oriental Art), New Delhi
*Marg* (A Magazine of Architecture and Art), Bombay
*Oriental Art*, Oxford
*Transactions of the Oriental Ceramic Society*, London
*Wên Wu* (Journal of Chinese Culture), Peking
*Wên-wu tsan-k'ao tze-liao* (Reference Material on Chinese Culture), Peking